Towards a New Enlightenment –
The Case for Future-Oriented Humanities

The book series "THE NEW INSTITUTE.Interventions" aims at strengthening the voice of the humanities in public and political discourse. Its publications present the work of the fellows of THE NEW INSTITUTE, based in Hamburg, which brings together changemakers from academia, activism, the arts, media, government, and business to collectively generate new ideas and solutions for the most pressing problems facing humanity today. By linking up such diverse perspectives and mindsets in a highly collaborative effort, THE NEW INSTITUTE strives to create fresh, groundbreaking approaches for tackling some of the most complex challenges of our time. Through such a collectively produced body of knowledge that includes both astute analyses and fundamental reconfigurations in various key areas of society, our "Interventions" will hopefully provoke and fuel constructive debates across disciplinary and sectoral boundaries. All texts in the series are published Open Access under a CC license to facilitate the widest possible reach for these conceptual and practical impulses.

Towards a New Enlightenment – The Case for Future-Oriented Humanities

Markus Gabriel, Christoph Horn, Anna Katsman, Wilhelm Krull,
Anna Luisa Lippold, Corine Pelluchon, Ingo Venzke

[transcript]

THE NEW
INSTITUTE

Bibliographic information published by the Deutsche Nationalbibliothek
The Deutsche Nationalbibliothek lists this publication in the Deutsche Nationalbibliografie; detailed bibliographic data are available in the Internet at http://dnb.d-nb.de

First published in 2022 by transcript Verlag, Bielefeld
© Markus Gabriel, Christoph Horn, Anna Katsman, Wilhelm Krull, Anna Luisa Lippold, Corine Pelluchon, Ingo Venzke

Cover layout: Maria Arndt, Bielefeld
Copy-editing: Joan Lace, Saffron Walden
Layout (adaptation) and typeset: Michael Rauscher, Bielefeld
Printed by Friedrich Pustet GmbH & Co. KG, Regensburg
Print-ISBN: 978-3-8376-6570-3
PDF-ISBN: 978-3-8394-6570-7
EPUB-ISBN: 978-3-7328-6570-3
https://doi.org/10.14361/9783839465707
ISSN of series: 2751-9619
eISSN of series: 2751-9627

Contents

Preface

In many respects our world is out of balance. The gaps are widening between technological advancements and social progress, between economic success and environmental degradation, and between research-based insights and political decision-making. They are complemented by a rapid loss of biodiversity, a growing trend towards privatization and commercialization of common goods, and last but not least by growing inequality, uncertainty, and complexity involved in meeting the challenges ahead of us.

When we look at the current state of affairs, the mounting crises, the Russian–Ukrainian war, and the atrocities that go with it, we surely have many reasons to give in to feelings of pessimism and despair. The downward spiral of adverse developments appears to dominate our perception. And yet, as scholars as well as concerned citizens we can no longer ignore the fact that it is the responsibility of our generation to come up with new ideas and viable concepts that can pave the way for an urgently needed transformation of our lifestyles, modes of production, and societies at large.

By courageously, critically, and creatively reflecting on various imbalances and their root causes as well as by trying to open up pathways to viable solutions for at least some of the huge problems we are confronted with, scholars and practitioners from various walks of life can help to change course in the direction of a more just, ecologically sound, and economically sustainable future. This holds particularly true when they jointly embark upon a journey focused on thoroughly rethinking and reconfiguring current practices.

TOWARDS A NEW ENLIGHTENMENT ■ MARKUS GABRIEL, CHRISTOPH HORN, ANNA KATSMAN, WILHELM KRULL, ANNA LUISA LIPPOLD, CORINE PELLUCHON, INGO VENZKE

7

It is against this background that the first cohort of fellows at THE NEW INSTITUTE involved in the start-up phase of our programme *'Foundations of Value and Values'* set out to develop a conceptual and strategic framework for an intellectually ambitious attempt at positioning the humanities in the wider context of bringing about systemic change. Despite the professional diversity of the group, fellows succeeded in focusing on their commonalities alongside their differences. This discussion paper is itself proof of the integrative capacity of the humanities. Building on their epistemic foundations and specific expertise, as well as their boldness and persistence, the humanities will nevertheless have to enlarge the scope and scale of their activities beyond understanding past and present phenomena towards more future-oriented approaches.

All of this requires a change of perspectives not only within the humanities themselves but also in the respective ecosystems of knowledge production at large. Even nowadays, in many debates focusing on research and innovation agendas, the humanities are often seen as less useful when it comes to shaping the future. While science and engineering are widely accepted as the key drivers of economic and technological progress, the humanities seem to lack a clear orientation towards the major challenges ahead of us. This perception of a set of decoupled knowledge domains urgently needs to be changed, last but not least in view of the multiple, interwoven crises we are confronted with.

To ultimately realize their potential as strongholds of reflexivity, multi-perspectivity, and normativity, the humanities will have to proactively take on the task of adopting a conceptual and strategic framework that puts them centre stage when it comes to tackling such crucial questions for our common future as: What is a sustainable value system for the 21st century? How can we create a common way forward towards a New Enlightenment? When and why are people prepared to change their behaviour and to reconfigure their lifestyles in favour of a sustainable future for humankind and our planet? Last but not least, the provision of adequate answers to these questions will require serious commitment to interdisciplinary, trans-sectoral, and intergenerational collaboration.

In several respects this was the spirit in which our fellows – namely Markus Gabriel, Christoph Horn, Anna Katsman, Corine Pelluchon, and Ingo Venzke – cooperatively and creatively worked

THE NEW
INSTITUTE

on this paper. My deeply felt thanks go to all of them and to Anna Luisa Lippold as well as Barbara Sheldon from the facilitating team for their impressive and continued commitment to our common endeavour.

In addition, many distinguished colleagues provided helpful comments on an earlier draft or discussed selected parts with us. These include Ruth Chang, Lorraine Daston, Nikita Dhawan, Rainer Forst, Hans-Ulrich Gumbrecht, Geoff Mulgan as well as Martin Adjei, Harald Atmanspacher, Isabel Feichtner, Tobias Müller, Vladimir Safatle, and Christiane Woopen. Their criticisms and supportive arguments considerably improved our manuscript, in particular with a view to explaining our request for more future-oriented humanities as well as possible options for working our way towards a New Enlightenment. Moreover, we thank the participants of the TNI@Stanford meeting organized by Markus Gabriel on 3–4 March 2022, who provided further comments and significant input: Andrea Capra, Amir Eshel, Roland Greene, Hans-Ulrich Gumbrecht, Robert Pogue Harrison, Courtney Blair Hodrick, Paul Kottman, Teathloach Wal Nguot, and Laura Wittman.

We are also grateful to Karin Werner and her colleagues at transcript publishing house, first and foremost for their enthusiasm about our aspirations and our project, but also for their invaluable support in the production and distribution process of this booklet.

Last but not least, I would like to thank our generous founder and funder Erck Rickmers for his friendship, empathy, care, and courage in all matters of concern to our joint endeavours at THE NEW INSTITUTE and beyond.

Wilhelm Krull
Founding Director of THE NEW INSTITUTE

Hamburg, July 2022

TOWARDS A NEW ENLIGHTENMENT ▪ MARKUS GABRIEL,
CHRISTOPH HORN, ANNA KATSMAN, WILHELM KRULL,
ANNA LUISA LIPPOLD, CORINE PELLUCHON, INGO VENZKE

9

1 The need to recouple the humanities and social sciences with society

Humanity is facing a complex meshwork of nested crises: the ecological crisis, various economic crises (from financial crises to growing inequalities), the geopolitical crisis, the energy crisis, the soon to be massive migration crisis fuelled by geopolitical catastrophes, the crisis of healthcare, and the still ongoing coronavirus crisis. These crises are systemic, global, and experienced by different human and non-human actors in a variety of ways. They confront us with environmental, economic, health, social, and political risks, which raise profound questions about the currently dominant models that define what is perceived as successful and normatively desirable development.

A crisis does not just mean that something is wrong or that there is a general problem or even a very big problem. A crisis, from the Greek *krisis*, means a decision; a crisis is a turning point that requires an intervention in order to avoid *catastrophe*. A crisis is, thus, a normatively laden turning point. Its outcome depends on human decision-making in conditions of social and natural complexity. For this reason, we can only meaningfully deal with a crisis by endorsing a set of normative principles from different domains in order to prevent catastrophe by taking the right decisions.

However, the current crises are all interwoven and they are associated with different kinds of normativity: military and ethical, ecological and economic, legal and aesthetic, cultural and universal, local and global, individual and collective norms are at play both in describing and in solving the problems that first lead to crisis and, if unresolved, transform into catastrophe.

One important driver of the dynamics of the nested crises noted above is the *decoupling* of natural-scientific, technological, and economic development from broader questions of human value, the good life, and wellbeing.[1] A few examples may suffice to illustrate this point:

TOWARDS A NEW ENLIGHTENMENT ■ MARKUS GABRIEL,
CHRISTOPH HORN, ANNA KATSMAN, WILHELM KRULL,
ANNA LUISA LIPPOLD, CORINE PELLUCHON, INGO VENZKE

11

- The immense power of modern information and communication technology (most recently: artificial intelligence) in large-scale social systems is restructuring human interaction in hitherto unknown ways. Purely technological perspectives cannot answer the question of the purposes to which technology should be put, and who is entitled to make such decisions.[2] The risk is that human value, collective decision-making, and wellbeing will be left behind. For this reason, governments rightly call for the regulation of socially disruptive information and communications technology in legal and ethical terms, which is why the recent discipline of the 'ethics of AI' has gained much attention. Its function is to re-couple socially disruptive technology with research into legal and ethical values and value representations in order to provide guidelines for how to reshape the relevant technology in light of human needs, rights, and duties.
- The digital transformation called for by many governments as part of the solution to the ecological crisis in turn creates novel issues of sustainability as a result of the material resources needed to produce and maintain the material dimensions of apparently purely symbolic data. The humanities are ideally suited to critically investigate this ideological layer and the illusions generated in a context of rapid social transformation. Recoupling in this context means integrating humanistic and social-scientific qualitative studies into the discourse of digital transformation with the aim of distinguishing between desirable and undesirable cases of automation of labour and replacement of human interaction and practices by digital systems.
- Food production and consumption are driven by unsustainable desires, expectations, and mindsets. Inappropriate mindsets hamper the ability to tackle the complex relationship between humans, non-human animals, and our shared habitat so that a systemic change on the level of mindsets and their material conditions is necessary. The humanities deal with our view of ourselves as

THE NEW
INSTITUTE

human beings. Insofar as human beings do what they do in light of broad conceptions of how they fit into nature, how they share features with non-human animals while still being profoundly different from them, humanistic research into such conceptions and mindsets is a precondition for meaningful, systemic change of our value representations.

- Standard economic models that still focus predominantly on quantitative growth are too narrow to measure human wellbeing. This leads to a conception of the socio-economic sphere in ways largely blind to the models designed to explain and overcome shortcomings in the actual target system of economic models, i.e. our economies. The very discipline in the business of producing economic solutions creates new problems when it does not take value-laden human experience into account in its efforts to measure economic success. Unrealistic conceptions of us as human beings, of our preferences, utilities, mindsets, desires, and modes of thinking and cooperating affect concrete policy proposals which then interfere with society as the broadest domain of socio-economic interaction. Socio-economic interactions qua target-systems of economics contain values and value representations in the form of the arts, religion, vast cultural differences, local and global histories, as well as threats, hopes, and interests on individual and collective levels that have to be integrated into economic theory. The humanities, therefore, can and ought to contribute to a paradigm change in economic thinking which takes into account the concepts of the quality of life, the first-person perspective of human agents and their integration into larger natural and social processes.

A false self-conception has negative consequences for how we act. Thus, the positive contribution of humanistic self-investigation into how we conceive of ourselves at various levels of individual action and social interaction consists in correcting false consciousness. This requires transdisciplinary cooperation, i.e. academic research

TOWARDS A NEW ENLIGHTENMENT ▪ MARKUS GABRIEL,
CHRISTOPH HORN, ANNA KATSMAN, WILHELM KRULL,
ANNA LUISA LIPPOLD, CORINE PELLUCHON, INGO VENZKE

13

across disciplinary boundaries that takes place in a context of so-cio-economic interaction with stakeholders and practitioners from all relevant fields.

Reorienting the humanities and social sciences

The globally interconnected, nested crises – produced and experi-enced differentially across nations, geographies, and sectors – call for a shift in the value structures and value representations that are among the sources of these crises. To the extent that humans act in light of a conception of themselves, they produce value representa-tions. For humans lead a life on the basis of what they deem valu-able. These value representations are not natural givens, as written in our DNA, but products of histories. The humanities study value representations and are able to discuss them in light of normative principles generated in ethics, economics, theology, and the law, to name but a few examples.

Value representations, thus, can be evaluated in light of actual values, be they constructed or produced by human action (as value constructivists assume) or detected due to a special human capacity for making sense of our value-laden experience of the life-world (as some value phenomenologists and moral realists argue).

The values that tacitly underpin ecologically unsustainable, and socially unjust economic as well as political practices and decision-making need to be brought to light, interrogated, and changed. If the transition to a more sustainable lifeworld takes place without integrating value structures and representations into its ethos, the decoupling problems which landed us in the modern predicament are likely to tighten.

The massive shifts human beings are beginning to experience as a species in the face of climate change raise new questions of how to value natural goods, environments, and animals, as well as the sta-tus of our ethical obligations to one another as denizens of a planet with limited natural resources. How to determine and distribute re-sponsibility for the production and solution of problems depends, among other things, on social and historical parameters grounded in different conceptions of the human condition and its integration into the cosmos. This means that future-oriented research from the humanities can and ought to be integrated into other knowledge and practice fields which already deal with how to tackle systemic crises,

THE NEW
INSTITUTE

often neglecting humanistic insights due to the institutional decoupling we describe above.

The inevitable socio-ecological transformation underway is, thus, in urgent need of a humanistic and social underpinning. In this regard, we call for a future- and goal-directed positioning of research to develop conceptual tools that can contribute to a new 'Vision of the Good' (Leiter 2013: 121).

Today this goes beyond a culture of individual practical wisdom. For what is at stake in complex crises is *social* and not merely *individual* freedom. Social freedom concerns the shape of meaningful activities which only make sense against a background of shared understanding. Where social freedom is concerned, community and the individual reciprocally determine one another. Individual self-determination has to be reconfigured in light of collective responsibility. For this reason, we ought to reconcile the moral demands on individual action with the collective architecture of the very problem space within which our individual choices make sense. Both have to be taken into account, which requires a new form of intellectual cooperation across the humanities and social sciences as well as feedback loops to and from non-academic actors. Interdisciplinary exchange is not enough; we need trans-sectoral cooperation and integration in order to shift our mindsets and structure social change in light of our 'best account' (Rosa 2021: 151) of what it means to be human in the 21st century.[3]

---

2   The unique knowledge position of the humanities and social sciences

Human beings are 'self-interpreting animals' (Taylor 1985: 45–76). This implies: How we make sense of ourselves shapes who we are and who we become. There is no single substantial nature to the human in light of which we can identify stable sets of preferences or patterns of societal wellbeing. Human beings have the higher-order ability to select rules, maxims, guiding principles, and normative

TOWARDS A NEW ENLIGHTENMENT ■ MARKUS GABRIEL,
CHRISTOPH HORN, ANNA KATSMAN, WILHELM KRULL,
ANNA LUISA LIPPOLD, CORINE PELLUCHON, INGO VENZKE

15

self-images for their agency. They are also capable of making their value-laden experience explicit by formulating theories based on value representations. These value representations can be assessed as correct or incorrect. This is the basic idea of practical normativity, i. e. of norms inherent to our social practices.

One can think of the humanities as contributing to the heuristics of ethical insight. By describing human experience in a transcultural and multi-perspectival setting, they inform us about deep cultural and mental differences of individuals and collectives. We thus need humanistic knowledge in order to advance ethics and other normative disciplines that put the human being centre stage.

One way of characterizing the unique knowledge position of the humanities can be specified with recourse to an 'indispensability thesis' (Gabriel 2020b: 3),[4] that is, the thought that the gigantic array of subjective positions from which human beings experience reality is indispensable to knowledge of the human. There is no calculus that would allow us to replace discussions concerning right ends with technocratic solutions. For this reason, human becoming cannot adequately be represented by providing ever more technical or technocratic answers to our problems. Human existence is fundamentally value-laden so that a value-driven approach in the humanities and social sciences cannot be circumvented.

Humanistic knowledge differs from the instrumental use of reason in that it is deeply concerned with describing synchronically and diachronically varying self-conceptions of human beings. Humanistic insight which draws on cultural, symbolic artefacts (including, but not limited to artistic, religious, and other modes of value expression) can, thus, contribute to a heuristics for ethics.[5] If there is a difference between value representations and actual values, i. e. if there is any kind of minimal objectivity to normative debates, there is a need for a methodology of normative disciplines and we propose to think of the humanities as being in a position to contribute their already developed methods to the goal of specifying conditions for positive social change. Their results and insights can thereby contribute to empirical research in the social sciences which in turn will actively shape social change in tandem with humanistic inquiry.

Insofar as the symbolic order shapes our behaviour even under urgent conditions (such as a pandemic or the climate crises we are facing), we cannot even understand, let alone change, how we are acting without enlisting the humanities to contribute their analyses to a description and reorientation of our action space. As the poet and cultural critic Bayo Akomolafe put it during his keynote speech at a recent workshop on 'objectivity in the humanities': 'The times are urgent; let us slow down' (Forum Humanum 2021, at 1:26:35).

Getting values into view requires that scholars from the wide range of the humanities and social sciences participate in the production, reproduction, and discovery of values. The humanities and social sciences implicitly and explicitly render value judgements. The value judgements cannot be reduced to the value representations which circulate in 'society' anyway. Rather, they are grounded in scholarly, systematic, and methodological knowledge-acquisition characteristics of the manifold disciplines rightly grouped together in virtue of their specific epistemic position.

Many of our most urgent, concrete, and practical questions are, upon closer look, questions addressed by the humanities and social sciences. Existential threats to humanity prompt questions about how humans should relate to nature. They have shaken bedrock beliefs about how the economy should be organized. They call for solidarity in a world of stark divisions. The humanities and social sciences have started to respond, and we can connect to those developments to further bridge the gap between them and society at large.

There are many proposals in play on how to respond, for instance, to climate change, ranging from geo-engineering solutions to interrogating the ethics of production and consumption practices. How are we to evaluate these proposals and which should we prioritize? Who is qualified to make these decisions and why? These are interpretive and not just political power questions that require public dialogue facilitated and supported by specialists in values and value representations working on these issues.

For instance, trained humanists working in the rapidly developing field of ecocriticism address questions like: are apocalyptic, hellscape stories of impending climate doom the right or good stories to be told? Why are we telling these stories to ourselves? Is the nature of climate change best represented, from an imaginative and affective point of view, in quantitative terms such as '1.5 degrees'? Is shaping the problem through thick notions of guilt and sacrifice compatible with the motivational sets through which human beings actually change their fundamental behaviours? Just as technology and the natural sciences help us build infrastructure such as roads and computers, the humanities provide the infrastructure for asking and addressing questions like the above.

As self-conscious, social beings *we cannot but make sense of how we make sense*. Despite the continuing rise of a consumerist or entrepreneurial notion of the self, people continue to seek and make meaning and self-understanding. Debates about truth and objectivity in a world of fake news and 'alternative facts', the relationship between individuality and community, our responsibilities to one another, non-human life forms, the earth, and more, cannot but continue; whether this will be done in a rigorous, sensitive, nuanced way, and lead to results, depends on how central the study of humanities remains in our culture. As Martha Nussbaum puts it:

> Responsible citizenship requires... a lot more [than learning the basic techniques of economics]: the ability to assess historical evidence, to use and think critically about economic principles, to assess accounts of social justice, to speak a foreign language, to appreciate the complexities of the major world religions. The factual part alone could be purveyed without the skills and techniques we have come to associate with the humanities. But a catalogue of facts, without the ability to assess them, or to understand how a narrative is assembled from evidence is almost as bad as ignorance, since the pupil will not be able to distinguish ignorant stereotypes purveyed by politicians and cultural leaders from the truth, or bogus claims from valid ones. World history and economic understanding, then, must be humanistic and critical if they are to be at all useful in forming intelligent citizens, and they must be taught alongside the study of religion and of philosophical theories of justice. Only then will they supply a useful foundation for the public debates that we must have if we are to cooperate in solving major human problems. (Nussbaum 2016: 93–94)

THE NEW INSTITUTE

3 The methods of the humanities and social sciences

Against this background, we wish to disclose the already existing potential of the humanities and social sciences to create meaningful contributions to trans-sectoral research regarding the urgent challenges of the 21st century. By repositioning the humanities and social sciences in context, our aim is to reconfigure as well as to expand all the solutions drawn by current debates. In need of fundamentally new ideas as well as reshaped concepts, scholarly research generally requires a deeper ability to reflect on itself, its methods, the interaction between disciplines, as well as its connectivity to other sectors of society (politics, business, the arts, civil society) and their specific needs. Taking responsibility for co-creating approaches to viable solutions requires complementing the stage of social critique (without ignoring its analytical tools) with constructive contributions that draw positive as well as captivating imaginaries. This imaginary must always start from a critical analysis and questioning of prevailing problem descriptions. And when it comes to unfolding innovative perspectives, establishing a high-trust culture of creativity – individually and institutionally – is key.

Broad concept of humanities and social sciences

Historically, the humanities and social sciences have evolved based on socially accepted modes of shaping one's character. They originate from attempts to make the principles of character formation explicit in the form of rules of wisdom, catalogues of virtues, as well as literary and artistic representations of socially important affairs.

Of course, what we call 'the humanities and social sciences' originates and develops in different ways depending on local histories and value representations. Thus, there are as many histories of those disciplines as there are systematic attempts to make the foundational values of a given social order explicit by way of symbolic representation. We note, however, that some alternative knowledges have been glossed over to the extent that the so-called subaltern has been

TOWARDS A NEW ENLIGHTENMENT ■ MARKUS GABRIEL,
CHRISTOPH HORN, ANNA KATSMAN, WILHELM KRULL,
ANNA LUISA LIPPOLD, CORINE PELLUCHON, INGO VENZKE

19

denied the means – the categories of representation – to speak and be heard,[6] leading to a situation of 'hermeneutical injustice'.[7]

The idea that there is *value-knowledge* and *wisdom* which differs from physical or natural-scientific knowledge concerning anonymous, material-energetic processes in the cosmos (i.e. anti-reductionism) has been a decisive component in the development of the humanities. When, in Athenian democracy of the 5th century BC, the need for the education of well-informed citizens arose in what would later become Europe, philosophers and political thinkers started to discuss appropriate educational programmes. Thus, democracy in Athens promoted learning and innovation to an extent hitherto unknown.[8] The curricula under discussion were not confined to intellectual skills, but included what has been called 'virtue of character'.[9] The personal ideal individuals had to pursue was *kalokagathia*, a term that combines outstanding intellectual competence with several further desirable character traits. In this original context, the humanities and the social sciences (such as economics and politics, as developed by Aristotle) serve the function of developing virtues, and thereby foster the ethical life of society. This is not only true of the humanities and social sciences in the so-called 'West'. Systematic ways of achieving wisdom, social stability, and prosperity were developed in Chinese and Indian contexts as well as in the complex histories of the African continent that heavily influenced the development of a scholarly attitude towards nature and human beings via the Egyptian paradigm.

Virtue ethics and its educational programmes later produced models of a 'comprehensive formation' (*enkuklios paideia*, an expression that survived in our word 'encyclopedia') and 'liberal arts' (*artes liberales*). Certain disciplines were considered 'free' in the sense of being valuable for free citizens and their happiness; as Aristotle described it, *sophia* (wisdom) is this type of knowledge since, being about 'first principles', it is valuable in itself, not for further purposes. It thereby becomes the prototype of the very idea of an end in itself, something intrinsically valuable.

A form of value-knowledge irreducible to the kind of objective knowledge we possess concerning nature stands at the core of each *emancipatory* movement that aims to foster personal autonomy and social freedom alike. In the so-called Western tradition, we can speak of a 'Greek enlightenment' as the source of the humanities.

While Aristotle and many of his contemporary scholars believed that slavery was an inevitable aspect of a free society and that women were morally deficient, emancipatory knowledge has progressed over the millennia. One of the forces of moral and human progress has been precisely the emancipatory knowledge stemming from the humanities and social sciences – more recently by pointing out the need to decolonize many of our assumptions about human becoming, which is an important element for viable accounts of universalizing in the 21st century. To be sure, moral progress has never been steady, linear, or unequivocal, nor is it anywhere near its end. The fruits of actual emancipatory imagination and knowledge certainly have not been fully realized, as ongoing humanistic debates and social-scientific research concerning systemic racism, hidden slavery, explicit misogyny, and social violence in contexts of 'race', sex, gender, class, national identity, and so forth clearly demonstrate.[10]

From Aristotle to Hannah Arendt, the humanities have drawn on considerations concerning practical reason *(phronesis)*. Phronesis is a term for the context-sensitive faculty of goal-setting and goal-pursuing that takes into account a wide range of values and facts, life conditions, and accidental circumstances, and connects them with the good or happy life of humans *(eudaimonia)*. The false ideology of today's *homo oeconomicus* appears today as a 'rational fool'[11] since he neglects his deeper and wider interests in life – an insight widely recognized in economics, which has realized that human agency is profoundly shaped by morally relevant value representations irreducible to an articulation of individual preferences. *Phronesis*, by contrast, is conceived of as an ability to provide a comprehensive rational orientation on goods and evils and to rightly prioritize them. The prudent person (the *phronimos*) thereby develops a global overview encompassing what is good for the city as a collective locus of social self-determination and autonomy.

In a more technical sense, the humanities began to develop specific methods designed to make their knowledge acquisition objectively shareable during the Hellenistic period. The method adopted for understanding the Homeric epics was based on Aristotle's idea of 'epistemic pluralism'. This is part of the genealogy of hermeneutic methods of understanding cultural and mental differences encoded in both oral and literal modes of expression. As Aristotle claims, we are not entitled to reduce all cognitively valuable procedures to

TOWARDS A NEW ENLIGHTENMENT ■ MARKUS GABRIEL,
CHRISTOPH HORN, ANNA KATSMAN, WILHELM KRULL,
ANNA LUISA LIPPOLD, CORINE PELLUCHON, INGO VENZKE

21

a single methodological standard (to the standard nowadays associated with the dominant Anglophone meaning of 'science' as technoscience). Instead, we should rather acknowledge that the epistemic standards for, e.g., mathematical proofs, logical arguments, poetological analysis of literary works of art and morally valid norms are highly different. In the case of textual interpretations, one must apply a method that carefully takes into consideration linguistic deviations, historical diversity, and the nature of the human being (emotions, desires, needs, attitudes, virtues, and vices, etc.).

In the modern German-speaking context, Friedrich Schleiermacher and Wilhelm Dilthey coined the conceptual dichotomy between explaining *(Erklären)* and understanding *(Verstehen)*, which can be interpreted as a distinction between two complementary modes of relating to reality.[12] Whereas the former characterizes scientific methods designed to identify nomological regularities in 'natural' reality independent of mind, language, and theory, the latter contextualizes historical documents by locating them in their original sphere. One of Dilthey's most relevant contributions to hermeneutics (the theory of understanding and self-understanding) is his description of the culturally shared sphere in which individuals are embedded from their earliest childhood. Understanding the details of a given historical text means grasping this sphere and integrating its details into a coherent narrative.

This hermeneutical approach of the humanities was further developed by Max Weber. Weber formulated an action theory emphasizing that to understand something is to place it in a 'context of meaningfulness' *(Sinnzusammenhang)*. For this reason, the humanities and the social sciences are deeply interwoven in that they take value representation and value judgements into account without thereby immediately accepting them as objectively valid.[13]

It was Edmund Husserl who, in the late 1920s, coined the concept of 'lifeworld' *(Lebenswelt)*, which plays a prominent role in contemporary social thought.[14] On its basis, Husserl was able to unify his phenomenological theories of the experience of consciousness of space, time, other minds, the body, etc. Finally, we have in Heidegger, Gadamer, and Ricœur, fully fledged philosophical standpoints based on the hermeneutical idea of understanding human existence. These philosophers leave behind the Husserlian idea of transcendental subjectivity and adopt a thoroughly historical paradigm of the human life form. They attack a description of human existence which takes a theoretical attitude towards the world as our primary view.[15]

All these standpoints attribute a privileged role to the humanities vis-à-vis our capacity to lead our lives in light of a conception of ourselves.[16] For them, only the humanities can provide a non-reductive picture of our lives and of human becoming based on specific methods designed to make sense of our human sensemaking in its social and historical context.

To be sure, there is a multitude of histories of the humanities and social sciences that are entangled with each other. Humanistic concepts travel, in a way that often reflects balances of power, across continents and disciplines. Making this explicit is part and parcel of the methods of the humanities.[17] All intellectual traditions emerging from the axial age and its preconditions in *longue durée* oral histories provide us with ways to discuss existential issues of human life.

Need for value-laden approaches

The methods of the humanities, as we find them, can be integrated into normatively guided social change through the idea that they are instrumental in figuring out value facts. For the human standpoint, subjectivity is vital to any account of experience which underpins claims to political participation.

It is a mistake to draw a sharp ontological line between facts and values. Max Weber was one of the authorities who introduced the idea of such a separation in order to keep empirical social sciences free from evaluative judgements that presuppose, as he believed, certain subjective ideological, political, or religious standpoints. In his influential papers on the 'Objectivity of Social Sciences and Socio-political Knowledge'[18] and his 'Science as Vocation',[19] Weber formulated his plea for value-free research that should pave the way for politicians to make, in a second, independent step, value-based decisions. The task of the social scientist is then restricted to the identification of facts; it is not to give concrete advice by making specific normative recommendations. Weber saw it as impossible to speak of moral values in an objective and neutral sense – whereas our assumption is that value-driven forms of research in sciences and humanities do not undermine their objectivity but simply cannot (and should not) be avoided.

The sharp distinction between facts and values is usually traced back to David Hume. As Hume claimed, no valid normative conclusion can be derived from a set of factual premises. For quite a long time, Hume's Is–Ought-problem (also known as Hume's guillotine) has been seen as dividing reality into two disjointed realms. According to this view, there exists no way to get from facts to values and vice versa. Facts are derived from a world-to-mind attitude, whereas values are in our minds and are applied to objects in a mind-to-world attitude.

But already in the early 1980s Hilary Putnam attacked the fact–value distinction in his influential book *Reason, Truth, and History*. He rejected the view that, since evaluative statements presuppose values, they can only be subjective.[20] He strongly supported the view that values can be the topic of objective debate, especially with regard to what the idea of 'human flourishing' implies.

Claiming the superiority of normative approaches over empirical ones is just as wrong as the opposite. Normative approaches are replete with factual assumptions and implicit causal claims. Conversely, no empirical inquiry is value-neutral, if only because it requires an account of what to look for and why. Questions relating to how empirical inquiry is conducted are also replete with normative choices and assumptions – and we don't mean only obvious examples of ethical limits to experiments. No facts 'carry their meaning along with themselves on their face' (Dewey 1954: 3). They require interpretation and the humanities for reflection and sensemaking. Reductionism must be avoided on all sides: Facts don't speak for themselves and yet they are more than projections of biases and normative preferences. Avoiding reductionism is a demand of scientific inquiry, of multi-disciplinarity, and of the need for radical societal change in view of overlapping crises.

The inevitability of value judgement is not only characteristic of the humanities and social sciences. It also applies to science and engineering. The reason why we focus on the humanities and social sciences here is not to exclude science and engineering, but rather to shift the level of observation and human activity from the field of intervening in natural processes by way of technology to the position of shifting mindsets. In a famous telegram from 1946, Albert Einstein wrote 'let the people know that a new type of thinking is essential if mankind is to survive and move toward higher levels'

THE NEW
INSTITUTE

(Nathan and Hordon 1960: 376). While he was speaking about the unleashed power of nuclear physics, the current crises are no less imminent (and still involve the issue of nuclear power). Changing mindsets in the right way for the sake of adjusting our behaviour and reconfiguring our institutions requires the kind of reflexive inquiry characteristic of the humanities and social sciences.

Pluralism of methods and approaches

The humanities and social sciences are sometimes seen as following a 'weaker' theoretical and methodological paradigm than the technosciences. But this judgement rests upon an early modern prejudice concerning the role of mathematics and experiential methods for the constitution of 'exact' sciences. Against such prejudices one should keep in mind the genuine diversity of epistemic fields – a diversity unearthed by humanistic disciplines such as the history of science or the sociology of knowledge. The insight that methods cannot simply be transferred from one domain to the other and that a researcher should stick to an appropriate method for a specific domain of objects can be traced back to Aristotle: he points out that the procedure adopted by a mathematician cannot be transmitted to the art of rhetoric and vice versa.

There is an old philosophical debate between epistemic monism and pluralism: while, on the one hand, Plato, Descartes, Leibniz, and philosophers and scientists associated with the Vienna School defended the idea that all epistemic methodologies can ultimately be reduced to one single procedural standard, one finds, from Aristotle to Nancy Cartwright and beyond, the idea that scientific disciplines and their methodologies cannot be unified. We think that monism implies a dangerous sort of reductionism that should be avoided, as it undermines the very idea of objectivity in the humanities and delegates value-knowledge to expressions of vital preferences or mere aesthetics. Given the contemporary state of the art in the natural sciences, the idea of subsuming all of them under some unified scientific view *(Einheitswissenschaft)* is fundamentally mistaken. The very idea of reducing humanistic, historically, and socially embedded value-knowledge and wisdom to the level of natural processes under investigation in 'science' is fundamentally misguided and certainly not grounded in actual scientific knowledge.

TOWARDS A NEW ENLIGHTENMENT ■ MARKUS GABRIEL, CHRISTOPH HORN, ANNA KATSMAN, WILHELM KRULL, ANNA LUISA LIPPOLD, CORINE PELLUCHON, INGO VENZKE

25

Decentring and multi-perspectivity

One of the major lessons of the various movements of critical theories in the last decades is that the humanities and social sciences make progress by decentralizing power positions that stabilize ultimately untenable forms of dualism and asymmetry based on privileging one polar extreme of a dualism. Deconstruction, postcolonial studies, disability studies, gender theories, post-structuralism, critical race theory, systems theory, and so forth have clearly demonstrated how knowledge fields are fanned out into a plurality of normative spheres governed by parameters such as power, economic interest, potentially harmful genealogies, biases, and social asymmetries. Eurocentrism, economism, ecocentrism, anthropocentrism, sinocentrism, and so forth designate untenable modes of organizing the relationship between highly complex normative spheres.[21] We accept these lessons as we move to a constructive, value-driven self-conception of the humanities and social sciences.

Any enterprise aiming to defend a project based on what we have in common, and which can be universalized, must have learned the lessons of history and know that any claim to define the good in a dogmatic way is prone to lead to the kind of violence it sets out to avoid. Thus, value judgements and objectivity in the humanities and social sciences is, of course, not insulated from fallibility and the possibility of correcting knowledge claims. Claims to knowledge must constantly reflect their relationship with power and its manifestation in belief systems and knowledge production. The value-laden investigation into a given set of value representations delivers defeasible claims. The defeasibility of claims to binding validity does not undermine but rather strengthens their objectivity. Claiming knowledge is not, as such, dogmatism.

Objective claims are precisely those which can be right or wrong. They need not be about objective matters in the sense of mind- and language-independent material-energetic reality. Objective judgement can have subjective experience as its target. In order to assess validity claims, humans need a community of diverse perspectives on the same facts so as to arrive at justified conclusions concerning what they actually know and ought to do. The defeasibility of knowledge claims in value domains, thus, amounts neither to the dogmatic defence of one's preferred narrative or prior commitments, nor to the kind of postmodern relativism and historicism

THE NEW
INSTITUTE

which challenges the very idea of knowledge in the normative domain.

The way in which we represent social affairs is always already value-laden. In that respect, there is no Archimedean point, no value-free 'view from nowhere' (Nagel 1989). Rather, following a recent proposal by Lorraine Daston and Peter Galison, we ought to think of the humanities and social sciences as striving for a view from everywhere.[22] Considered in this way, the humanities provide a systematic, methodological foundation for representing values. For, the target systems of their investigations are historically located expressions of values belonging to different layers of normativity. Their modes of knowledge-acquisition are irreducible to a value-neutral description of social affairs. In order to achieve this, new narratives must be the result of transcultural, trans-sectoral, and interdisciplinary cooperation. We might also say that the fact of every starting point being invariably partial does not mean that this is where one must end up.[23] The goal of a novel research and communication architecture is to face the global challenges of our planet head-on by bringing the humanities to the table.

The humanities have long dealt with multi-perspectivity in the following strong sense: Whereas the natural and technological sciences on many levels are perfectly entitled to think of their objects as for the most part independent of the mind, language, theory, society, and consciousness, the paradigmatic objects of the humanities are subjects and their integration into their symbolic communities. The humanities do not abstract from the full human perspective, but try to understand it in its social contexts. This means, among other things, that meaning and sensemaking themselves become objects of the humanities so that the idea that objectivity consists in simply mirroring nature or reality as it is, regardless of our intervention, turns out to be insufficient when we take the meaningfulness of human lives into account. We simply cannot study human meaning without engaging in it. Thus, the objects of the humanities are for the most part dependent on the mind, language, theory, society, and human consciousness. This has led to the insight that the nature–culture distinction is flawed – an insight consequential for the topic of an ecological transformation.[24] Even more specifically, the ecological humanities significantly contribute to a novel understanding of the humanities and their positive role for overcoming

TOWARDS A NEW ENLIGHTENMENT ■ MARKUS GABRIEL,
CHRISTOPH HORN, ANNA KATSMAN, WILHELM KRULL,
ANNA LUISA LIPPOLD, CORINE PELLUCHON, INGO VENZKE

27

various deadlocks of our time (such as apocalyptic and post-apocalyptic thinking).[25]

Universalism as universalization

While the very idea of universalism, like that of the human being, is all too easily associated with a static and essentialist position, what it aims at expressing is worth defending. Despite justified critiques of false universalisms,[26] whose falsity resides in confusing a local, particular norm of being human with a universal paradigm, universalism as such has not been shown to be a morally untenable position.[27] On the contrary, it is the ground on which legitimate concerns about Eurocentric, anthropocentric, or even racist justifications of colonialism and other forms of morally obnoxious exploitation stand. What moral progress has shown to be wrong and even evil is universally evil, regardless of the historical fact that some groups have been profiting from moral wrongdoing and systemic evil.[28]

In order to emphasize that tenable forms of universalism reject a static model of human nature according to which we would already be equipped with full reflexive self-knowledge and even entitled to automatically impose moral insight on those regarded as morally inferior, one ought to speak of universalizing. That is to say, the 'we' of the ethical community is open-ended and its construction is ongoing. As Xudong Zhang and Zhao Tingyang have pointed out, universalizing as a ground for claiming universality is certainly not limited to the European Enlightenment and, thus, historically not necessarily linked with a repression of otherness.[29]

Revitalizing hermeneutics

In general, *hermeneutics* is the theory of understanding and self-understanding. It has been developed in the context of the interpretation of texts and other cultural artefacts. In particular, its aim is to address diachronic, historical, but also synchronic cultural and overall mental differences between individuals, collectives, and cultures. Revitalizing hermeneutics today consists in bringing the methods of understanding cultural otherness to bear on the global issues we are facing. In order to see the humanity in each other's person (to borrow one of Kant's formulations of the Categorical Imperative), we have to understand the specific mode of becoming human. Human becoming is a series of self-interpretations. Humans realize the

THE NEW
INSTITUTE

form of being human in different ways. Revitalized hermeneutics, thus, presuppose the recognition of otherness as a starting point. Its goal is not to overcome otherness, but to see it as a resource in understanding the entanglement of universalism, humanism, and the contextuality of their realization.

From a hermeneutical perspective, the normative and the descriptive are intertwined, because the paradigmatic objects of hermeneutic investigation (holy scriptures, literary texts, artworks, legal texts) contain value representations that cannot be accessed from a value-free perspective (if there is such a thing in the first place).

Modern hermeneutics has been an important driver of different stages of enlightenment. Spinoza's hermeneutical criticism of the Bible forced scholars to pay attention to the different levels of the biblical texts and sub-texts. Similarly, Paul Ricœur has argued that we can think of Marx, Nietzsche, and Freud in terms of a 'hermeneutics of suspicion'.[30] Their genealogical methods allow us to understand how ideologies turn social into quasi-natural facts. Duncan Kennedy has diagnosed that such a hermeneutics of suspicion is the main mode for critiquing an opponent's legal argument, at least in the US context.[31] In international law, hermeneutics is similarly intertwined with realist critiques that are aimed at discrediting interpretations which do not achieve coherent self-reflexivity.

Revitalizing hermeneutics today means that we commit to the idea that horizons of meaning, sensemaking, and understanding are open and dynamic so that the fusion of horizons is not an exception, but the norm in global contexts where dialogue and mutual recognition of the legitimacy of a multiplicity of perspectives on complex issues are indispensable. This includes taking law, the arts, and religions seriously as media of self-expression that cannot and must not be reduced to the kind of modelling and theory construction constitutive of systems that can largely be explained in causal terms.

The phenomena that build the target system of the humanities are irreducibly qualitative. For this reason, the ethics of hermeneutics has always drawn on the Aristotelian idea of the quality of life as foundational for economics.[32] Revitalizing hermeneutics implies that quantitative methods from economics and other domains of social science which work with data sets as well as models of human thought and behaviour stemming from the natural sciences, ought to be integrated into the horizon of hermeneutics.[33] One hitherto

TOWARDS A NEW ENLIGHTENMENT ▪ MARKUS GABRIEL, CHRISTOPH HORN, ANNA KATSMAN, WILHELM KRULL, ANNA LUISA LIPPOLD, CORINE PELLUCHON, INGO VENZKE

29

largely unexplored option for future research and trans-sectoral cooperation would be to focus on qualitative rather than quantitative growth, i.e. to focus on practices of wisdom and humanistic self-knowledge in the actual design of economic indicators and policy-making.

While we endorse the idea of revitalizing hermeneutics, interpretation has its limits. As Gumbrecht and other leading humanists have pointed out, a controlled right to interpretation is embedded in socio-political contexts.[34] Even within the alleged 'ivory tower' of academic radical interpretation, there are rules of ethical discourse, fair allocation of resources, and acceptable limits of research. When put into words, interpretations face the strictures of narrative emplotments. No sphere of human action coordination is so radically autopoietic as to question absolutely all modes of practical human subjectivity. That also holds true for the interpretation of historical facts which are inevitably produced out of present contexts, desires, and theorizing, but mount stronger resistance to some particular interpretations. 'Objectivity [then] arises from comparing and criticizing rival webs of interpretations in terms of agreed facts' (Bevir 1994: 10).

Moral realism
One prominent option to thinking of the difference between value and value representation is moral realism, as a possible theory of moral value widely accepted by contemporary ethicists. In general, we can understand moral realism as the view that there are moral facts where a *moral fact* is a true answer to the question of what one ought or ought not do simply in virtue of our shared humanity. Articulation of our shared humanity is, thus, a decisive source of ethical insight. The anthropogenesis of ethical insight does not undermine the claims of animal and environmental ethics, but grounds them in our capacity to track moral facts, a capacity which is more evolved in humans than in any other known species. Moral facts are objective, which should not be understood as implying that they are mind-independent. For they concern us by virtue of being normative. Their normativity cannot be meaningfully reduced to the observable configuration of physical entities or observable human behaviour, as this would undermine their ethical status. Yet the fact that some facts involve human mindedness and social practices of recognition

does not undercut objectivity, as many uncritically assume is shown by the often overhasty rejection of the very idea of ethical objectivity.

Moral realism in that sense (which need not postulate metaphysically suspicious entities beyond the ken of human self-constitution) can be combined with the notion that we can derive ethical claims from the self-investigation of human agency and, therefore, practical subjectivity. As in Scanlon's book, 'what we owe to each other' can be articulated in the form of a theory of goods.[35] In this context, goods can be seen as ways of articulating the good. The good is a deontic necessity, something we ought to do under any circumstances. To the extent that human agency can only be actualized under certain, violable conditions, the good can be seen as a mode of *sustainability*: We ought to preserve the basic conditions of human agency and social action coordination, because it is the source of higher moral insight (ethics) through which the socially structured wellbeing of human and non-human actors (including the ecological niche we share with non-human animals) is promoted.

Ethics as a reflexive discipline is, thus, anthropogenic – elaborated by humans – without thereby being anthropocentric, that is, restricted to human utility. Value theory has long moved beyond the assumption that only humans deserve our care, concern, and attention. Our moral cognitions are not illusions or mere expressions of socially shared preferences, but rather reveal facts about human cooperation and our integration into the wider community of living beings. Thus, moral insight tracks moral facts which are not mysterious entities whose ontological status would be weak compared to measurable, physical quantities. In any event, denying the objectivity of ethical insight and the possibility of moral facts on the ground of a reductionist metaphysics according to which only the physical is real is an untenable stance, as it undermines any sort of value judgement, including judgements concerning value representations, as these cannot be translated into the vernacular of mathematical physics.

A dynamic form of moral realism is a fruitful approach to achieving a balance between universalism and historicity[36] that is at the heart of a New Enlightenment. It implies that there are moral facts concerning obligatory (good), neutral, and evil actions, which moral statements describe and whose existence and nature are partly independent of the beliefs of the people who express them.[37] These

TOWARDS A NEW ENLIGHTENMENT ■ MARKUS GABRIEL,
CHRISTOPH HORN, ANNA KATSMAN, WILHELM KRULL,
ANNA LUISA LIPPOLD, CORINE PELLUCHON, INGO VENZKE

31

moral facts provide guidelines to know what to do and what to forbid.

To be sure, these partly mind-dependent ethical reference points, which are powerful counterweights to relativism and nihilism, must be contextualized when passing from theory to practice, because conflicts occur when one moves from norm to application. We then face the cases and dilemmas characteristic of our times of uncertainty.[38]

This invites discussion, and in particular trans-cultural exchanges, as many moral facts are not obvious to individuals and collectives. Ethics too deals with uncertainty which arises at the interface of the complex web of normative orders,[39] to which it contributes a decisive level of inquiry.

In addition to the social complexity involved in the heuristics of values and value representation, moral facts are only partly mind-dependent. They involve the human life-form as a paradigmatic starting point that is nevertheless part of a larger natural environment which we share with other living beings. Moral facts are not isolated, purely 'cultural' artefacts; they are inextricably linked with the kinds of facts unearthed by natural science and implemented under economic conditions by technology. For this reason, a New Enlightenment requires large-scale cooperation across disciplines and cultures. The humanities and social sciences provide ethics with a heuristic for value judgement that copes with uncertainty and a full recognition of social complexity without committing the nihilistic or relativistic mistake of denying the existence of moral facts.

Moral constitutivism

Another prominent strategy to overcome the sharp facts–values separation has been developed by Christine Korsgaard in her version of *moral constitutivism*.[40] Korsgaard's basic idea is that our self-understanding as agents implies inescapable standards. These standards constitute human agency, which is, thus, value-laden as such. The descriptive constitutive elements of our agency contain, as its enabling conditions, at the same time substantive normative implications. Being an agent is, thus, an important source of moral insight. It does not take additional transcendent standards to achieve objectivity. Moral facts can, therefore, be seen as reflections of the constitutive aspects of agency and social cooperation. Moral constitutivists claim that, since we are not at liberty to select the foundations of our self-understanding as agents, it is also not up to us to accept or reject their implications. Normativity results from this inescapability.

Korsgaard and other moral constitutivists (e. g. David Velleman or Paul Katsafanas) claim that the gap between facts and values can thus persuasively be bridged with reflexive recourse to human agency. Therefore, the humanities are ideally suited to undertaking ethical investigations based on their specific, yet diverse methods and approaches.

A much-discussed argument elaborated by Korsgaard goes roughly as follows: Practical subjectivity relies on strictly binding normative preconditions. Part of these preconditions is that we are obliged to acknowledge certain goods as fundamental in that they turn out to be enabling conditions of our rational agency.

When raising the question of which goods we consider fundamental to our ability to act, we might, taking inspiration from Korsgaard's thought, arrive at the following list:

- *Psycho-physical goods*: these include basic elements of physical and psychic health such as being in (more or less) full possession of bodily faculties and living without permanent pain.
- *Mental goods*: these contain the faculty to use one's cognitive, volitional, imaginative, and emotional abilities, to grasp and follow values, to develop higher-order volitions and principles, and to carry out a life plan.
- *Social goods*: these encompass the goods of participation in social groups, the faculty to join such groups and to benefit from them: i. e. to enter close social relationships with partners, parents, children, relatives, friends, neighbours, colleagues, and so forth.
- *Political goods*: think here of a warranty of basic political rights (human rights, rights of participation, citizenship), the rule of law, benefiting from a positive political development in one's country, and from an open society, its educational system, and promotion prospects.
- *Economic goods*: standards of living and quality of life, including the educational system and the health-care system of a given nation state.

TOWARDS A NEW ENLIGHTENMENT ▪ MARKUS GABRIEL, CHRISTOPH HORN, ANNA KATSMAN, WILHELM KRULL, ANNA LUISA LIPPOLD, CORINE PELLUCHON, INGO VENZKE

33

- *Natural and environmental goods*: clean water, air, land, a biodiverse environment, access to healthy food, and the like.
- *Culture-dependent goods*: these are goods that are fundamental for being socially recognized in certain socio-historical contexts (as in the example of leather shoes and a white linen shirt in Adam Smith's *Wealth of Nations*).

These spheres have an objective impact on the good of rational autonomy that an individual can reach. It is possible to combine constitutivism and realism: The enabling conditions of human agency are part of an explanation for why there are moral facts. Thus, it is not our autonomous practical reason that discovers normative orders, but the historically embedded human being whose becoming is the object of humanistic investigation.

This approach to the fact–values dichotomy contains two further elements of interest. The first is that our inner desires and preferences (in general: our pro-attitudes) do not have any normative force unless they are accepted by the agent based on their 'reflective endorsement'. Thus, our evaluative judgement on actions is not simply an expression of our psychic life but is founded upon second-order reflections or normative self-images. To speak of an action, I must have affirmed and accepted certain 'pro-attitudes' to make them work; or, of course, I can reject them as inappropriate. Moreover, whatever motive I decide to follow, the decision must be based on reasons. These reasons guide my practical deliberation, and they must be 'internal'. In light of these reasons, the motives, impulses, or desires upon which I act must appear to me as justified. The second point is this: a reflective endorsement based on sufficient reasons to act is not suspended by the possible truth of what Korsgaard calls 'the scientific world-view' (Korsgaard 1996: 97) and not even by a possible causal determinism of agency. The 'space of reasons' in which I participate via my reflective endorsement cannot meaningfully be reduced to causes in the scientific sense. Here a facts–values distinction makes good sense: scientific facts (be they as real as it gets) do not imply a normative force.

Moreover, the practice of reflective endorsement cannot be adequately spelled out as a series of convenient, on-the-spot judgements. It must be formulated as a rule valid for all cases whose relevant features are similar. It is based on a practical identity harkening back to the agent's biographical background and socio-historical context: during the process of assessment and reflective endorsement, the agent is asked to replace given conditions with a consciously chosen normative self-image. My normative self-image then constitutes an obligation to act whenever my self-image would be damaged by inactivity or by acting differently. My chosen self-image is to be criticized in light of a dynamic concept of the broadest possible community of human becoming, humanity.

Phenomenology

A phenomenological approach can complement this perspective by starting with the suspension of our beliefs (*epoché*) and returning to the acts of consciousness which enable us to assess the meaning of things and of our relationships to them. Applied to our practices, this leads us to make an inventory: We can understand which practices deserve to be kept because they respect the meaning of the activities described and define which we must change or even suppress. This inventory, which has to be made at both the individual and collective level, is key to a process of emancipation involving both the liberation from counterproductive patterns and habits and the reorientation of our practices, i. e. taking back control over our lives, by saying what kind of world we want to live in and what we want to prevent.[41]

Hermeneutic phenomenology is a crucial part of humanistic methodology. Indeed it allows one to identify structures of existence that follow from the description of the human being understood as a historical being, endowed with freedom, and considered in their corporality as a vulnerable being who ages, dies, and needs others' care, and who 'lives from' natural and cultural things, or is dependent on nature and other living beings. Such a phenomenological anthropology that articulates the earthly, carnal, and relational dimension of the subject asks us to make the protection of the biosphere and justice towards other living beings and future generations novel duties of the state. The latter are added to the duties classically devolved to the political, namely our security and the reduction of unfair inequalities.[42]

Because phenomenology tries to get to the interaction between beings, human and non-human, and the world which they each

TOWARDS A NEW ENLIGHTENMENT ■ MARKUS GABRIEL,
CHRISTOPH HORN, ANNA KATSMAN, WILHELM KRULL,
ANNA LUISA LIPPOLD, CORINE PELLUCHON, INGO VENZKE

35

shape in their own way, it allows us to reveal several layers of lived experience. Given that human experience of social and natural reality is profoundly value-laden, the phenomenological, reflective understanding of the human life-world is an important methodological tool for the heuristics of ethics and other normative domains.

Underlining the heterogeneity of access to the world helps us understand that other animals shape the world in a different way to us and are other existences, as Merleau-Ponty describes it. There is one world, one planet, and a diversity of ways of configuring it. This 'lateral universalism' of which Merleau-Ponty speaks is the promise of a non-hegemonic rationalism.[43] The latter is not only welcoming of diversity, but shows that it is essential, since no one can have direct access to its totality; the process of discovering the world is open-ended.[44]

Narratives and values

After the tragedies of the 20th century, reason itself has come under attack: It can serve both good and evil, support any end, insofar as, having been reduced to its sole dimension of functionality and having been transformed into a force of calculation, it cannot by itself serve to distinguish good from evil, the just from the unjust.[45] The fall of the Berlin Wall, and the collapse of the communist ideal that gave people a horizon transcending their individual lives, have even banned political utopias from Western politics.[46] Instead, negative, dystopian, and apocalyptic modes of representing the future of humanity have conquered our social imagination, which is precisely part of our current situation vis-à-vis the nested crises we are in.

Postmodern discourse in the last quarter of the 20th century led the humanities to reject the idea of grand narratives. In the name of various dimensions of diversity, as we would nowadays call it, the humanities started to shy away from large-scale attempts to understand or even to shape social systems by providing positive narratives. Postmodern thinkers remained stuck in critical positions and thereby had too little to offer to counter the rapid rise of economism and promote a development model that is ecologically sustainable and more just.[47] Repudiating grand narratives as 'metaphysical' does not calm down the human desire to live a meaningful life. For this reason, other disciplines and actors have filled the gap left by the humanities and started constructing precisely the kind of grand narratives that postmodern thinkers deemed superfluous or even dangerous in view of the 'end of history', as Fukuyama (1989) puts it. Neoliberalism has been the most successful grand narrative to fill the gap: The idea that we need no narratives in order to globalize markets has itself become a grand narrative that is too often uncritically accepted as political dogma.

By now, it has become evident that the declaration of 'the end of history' and the end of large-scale narratives was premature. This explains the societal need for narratives and value-judgements that can contribute to positive social change. There have always been notable exceptions within the humanities and social sciences that have stayed closer to the demands of society. That has been the case for fragmented fields of applied ethics and for particular normative disciplines which have played a role in policy-advising, such as law or economics. There are signs that the situation is changing more generally. The digital revolution and developments in artificial intelligence have exposed the need for normative guidance and, in many research projects, put closer cooperation between researchers from a wide variety of backgrounds into practice. This is even more evident in the case of the ecological crisis, which stands at the centre of attention, and is a major source of the sense of urgency that characterizes our era of nested crises.

Whereas traditional wisdom was based on a cosmology allowing each one to know his place and to accept beliefs concerning what the good is, secular politics spread the belief that today we are ultimately 'alone, without excuses', as Sartre (2007: 29) put it in *Existentialism Is a Humanism*. Indeed, today we have no excuses, because our demographic weight, ecological footprint, and technological prowess make our human responsibility hyperbolic. At the same time, as many moral philosophers have argued, secular ethics is a rather young field of inquiry, as ethics has long been driven by various theological belief systems which are not universally shareable.[48] Secular ethics, as part of the humanities and social sciences, does not exclude religious spheres of normativity from consideration, as theology and religious studies (among other disciplines) explicitly deal with religious values and value representations, which are integrated into ethical value judgements without reducing them to any kind of divine revelation.[49]

TOWARDS A NEW ENLIGHTENMENT ■ MARKUS GABRIEL,
CHRISTOPH HORN, ANNA KATSMAN, WILHELM KRULL,
ANNA LUISA LIPPOLD, CORINE PELLUCHON, INGO VENZKE

37

Human decision-making is always driven by narratives. Humans project themselves into the future which is part of the very structure of human action. In this way, humans produce individual and collective narratives through which they make their historically and socially situated perspectives explicit and communicable. Confusing levels of normativity easily create false and socially harmful narratives. In a context of social complexity and thus of uncertainty, there is a strong temptation to cling to simplifying narratives – that is, to produce ideologies. The critical examination of given narratives is already a potential contribution to positive social change.

Humanistic recognition of a culture of genuine social complexity does not hinder action but can be factored into a non-reductive understanding of the human condition which we urgently need in order to tackle the global and therefore essentially multicultural conditions of production and reproduction of goods, services, thoughts, and experiences. New global solutions to the challenges ahead of us require overcoming the very idea of a centre of overall societal activity while bringing goals into focus.

Explanation of the characteristics of human action presupposes that we make recourse to narratives. On the individual level, humans think of their lives in light of their biographies to which they contribute by making choices. On the collective level, social identities are handed down as narratives from generation to generation by way of social imaginaries, cultural memories, mythologies, rituals, and so forth whose function is to provide overall normative guidelines. Narratives constitute dynamic identities thanks to which we anticipate the future as well as identify courses of action and existential possibilities open to us in the present.[50]

It is time to promote a self-conception of the humanities which allows them both to critically scrutinize various existing and competing large-scale narratives and to create new horizons of sense-making and meaning. Thinking about false narratives concerning socially important matters (such as social injustices of all sorts) can never occur in a value-free space.

Given the prominent role that the very idea of a narrative plays in contemporary socio-economic and political discourse formation, it is striking that its use is not yet tied to layers of normativity. Narratives can be better or worse, more or less useful; they can be judged by comparing them to the facts, thereby assessing the truth-value of some of their claims and how the claims add up to a plot-like, narrative structure of sensemaking.

We propose to think of the humanities as conceptual tools capable of sharpening the vague political notion of a narrative by providing multi-level conceptual and participatory tools in order to reconcile theory and practice. This implies that we ought to avoid a top-down approach according to which academic knowledge simply has to be transferred to other sectors of society. Rather, the methods, tools, and results that are developed in the humanities and social sciences have to be translated into different contexts, which requires substantial trans-sectoral cooperation that transcends 'business as usual':

1. On the *individual* level, narrative matters insofar as the narrative account of personal identity and subjectivity rightly represents a crucial dimension of agency. Humans lead a life in light of a conception of where they come from, who they are, and who they want to be. In this context, they tell stories that confer meaning on more specific actions, stories which provide a horizon of meaning. The humanities and social sciences (from literary and art criticism to political theory, from philosophy to sociology, from law to history, from sinology to media studies, and so on) in their broadest possible range of disciplines and activities provide understanding and explanation for how narratives are constructed on an individual level and how we ought to provide standards for assessing and evaluating them.

   These standards are not external to the subject matter of the humanities. Rather, the idea of a life led in light of the stories one tells about oneself is, as such, imbued with value; it offers its own normative self-conception. Yet narratives can succeed and fail in manifold ways. They can be manipulated, result from ideology and propaganda;[51] they can offer path-breaking and life-changing modes of solving problems, liberate an agent from fear, and significantly contribute to overcoming crises on an individual level (as is well known from the narratological architecture of psychoanalysis and other forms of psychological treatment).

TOWARDS A NEW ENLIGHTENMENT ■ MARKUS GABRIEL,
CHRISTOPH HORN, ANNA KATSMAN, WILHELM KRULL,
ANNA LUISA LIPPOLD, CORINE PELLUCHON, INGO VENZKE

39

2. On a *collective, social* level, narratives enter the picture in that groups organize themselves in light of fictional accounts of their being. To be social is to be integrated into storytelling, collective imagination, and acts of shared transcendence: The immediately given social setting is always transcended by any given group with respect to a shared (sometimes conflictual, sometimes positively coordinated) understanding of the focus of meaningful activity.[52]

   Regimes and institutions are eminent examples of such collectives. In the field of social and political sciences, thinking of nations as 'imagined communities', according to Anderson (2016), goes in a similar direction, and a constitution's preamble can be read as an expression of related stories about collective pasts and futures. Many transnational communities can be thought of as regimes, unified and distinguished by the legitimating narrative that is embedded in community practices.

3. In the ordering adopted here for the sake of exposition, the highest level of social identity formation is *humanity*. Humans can be regarded as the kinds of animals that constitutively lead a life in light of varying self-portraits. While individuals and collectives can differ in terms of their specific value representations, narratives, and goals (which is the basis of liberal pluralism as an indispensable parameter for all value formation), there is an overarching capacity, namely the capacity to specify one's individual or collective assumptions concerning the meaning of (human) life itself. Humans have a trans-cultural understanding of their capacity to be individu-als. Gabriel has called this 'higher-order anthropology' (Gabriel 2021: 65): All lower-level self-conceptions (such as the *homo oeconomicus, homo metaphysicus, homo ludens, pictor,* etc.) are grounded in the universal capac-ity to specify a human self-portrait.

   For our purposes, 'a narrative can be considered as a discursive form that opens semantic space for the integration and arrangement of a multiplicity of rep-resentations' (Gumbrecht 2004b: 23). At this point,

THE NEW
INSTITUTE

though, a well-known pitfall must be avoided. Engaging in the active humanist 'production of complexity' by considering multiple perspectives on processes of micro-, meso-, and macro-level social and ecological transformation should not mislead one into losing sight of the kinds of facts that are not open to change by interpretation. It would be a mistake to identify nature with this category of facts. Social and historical facts can be as 'unamendable'[53] and solid as geological facts, which is part and parcel of any explanation of the force of normativity. Normativity, and thus the source of values, is inextricably bound up with facts of human and non-human nature as well as with genealogical facts about the pasts, presents, and futures of social spheres.

Law and legal critique

Law, like art, plays a central role in society, enabling and constraining governance and everyday interaction. It shapes societies in their self-understandings through constitutions, the proclamation of values, public debate, and many transversal concepts such as those of sovereignty, the separation of powers, or citizenship. It is difficult to understand European society, for instance, were it not through the integrative capacity of law.[54] The law interacts with communities' broader processes of sensemaking, shaping society, and being shaped by it in the production of legal meaning. Law, Robert Cover averred with lasting impact, is 'not only a system of rules to be observed, but a world in which we live' (Cover 1983: 4–5).

Liberal democracies set up the law as a means for the individual and collective self-determination of realizing private and public autonomy, notably through contract and legislation. It would be a mistake to consider any law as static once written down, embedded with a meaning that could be revealed at any time. An understanding of law in analogy to the open-textured work of art, and of legal judgement in conversation with aesthetics, fares much better. Law provides the ground for struggles over its meaning in which subjective judgements compete for objectivity. In the operative legal discourse, the rules and canons of interpretation structure the justification for any judgement in distinct ways, and in an institutionalized system legal controversies can often be resolved through authoritative de-

TOWARDS A NEW ENLIGHTENMENT ■ MARKUS GABRIEL,
CHRISTOPH HORN, ANNA KATSMAN, WILHELM KRULL,
ANNA LUISA LIPPOLD, CORINE PELLUCHON, INGO VENZKE

41

cisions in court. But, for one thing, no interpretation or court judgement is entirely determined by the law and, for another, any court decision is again open to interpretation in a way that finds no end.

Under these conditions, legal critique can take many different forms.[55] Some interpretations of the law are still better than others *in terms of the law*. The open process of legal discourse cultivates a non-reducible layer of legal normativity. At the same time, presumptions of law's legitimacy can and should of course be critiqued and rebutted, in light of practical morality, in the spirit of a hermeneutics of suspicion, as ideology, or otherwise. The fact that the law is so closely tied to the workings of power just as well as to aspirations towards justice contributes to its central role in society. As such, the law shows traces of the best and the worst, taking stock of patterns of domination and struggles for emancipation at national, subnational and international levels of governance. Any critique raises questions about the standpoint of the critic, their situatedness and aspiration to objectivity. But neither the critic of law nor of art is alone in this, and the fact that every starting point of critique is partial does not mean that critique needs to end up there.[56]

---

4 The humanities and social sciences will only succeed if they pursue an integrative approach

Internal disciplinary dynamics and the organization of research have created obstacles for integrated approaches. Developments in research have paralleled the functional differentiation of society, leading to greater specialization and remarkable expertise. But they have come with the downsides of silos: deep but narrow views of the social world. Disciplinary identities and professional belonging have been constructed in negative opposition to respective others. The development of mainstream, allegedly value-free economics is only the most egregious example with its feeble attempt to rid itself of normative foundations.

The same may be said of parts of the humanities that have theorized in remarkable distance to facts. A practical philosophy without practice has a questionable standing, just like a legal theory that is ill-attuned to the operation of the law. Examples for both are too many. Factors supporting disciplinary self-isolation include career trajectories as well as the importance of journals that lead in rigorous rankings and are driven by methodological sophistication which might stifle creativity. Path-breaking interdisciplinary or multidisciplinary studies have of course been possible, but they are still too rare.

The humanities will only succeed in their endeavours if they can build bridges across cultures and continents based on the conviction that it is necessary to be aware of others, of the past, and of the path-dependencies of our present-day lives, if we want to responsibly shape the future. Past, present, and future ought to be connected in the historical temporalities in which we are embedded as situated subjects.[57]

Philological, historical, or philosophical approaches are often driven by close interactions between subject and object, the ones who try to understand and interpret, and the things to be interpreted. In a classic book, Theodor Litt emphasizes the importance of the will to be involved in shaping the future when it comes to analysing the present and its historical preconditions.[58] According to Litt, it is essential that the humanistic scholar approaches the objects of study in an unbiased, impartial, perhaps even objective manner, an approach 'full of self-denial' (Litt 1926: 413). The ability and the willingness to know more about the object of study needs to be closely associated with a firm basis in contemporary life. Otherwise, we will end up with a lot of mindless and meaningless notes.

In view of the opportunities as well as the limits and limitations of humanistic studies, it is essential to deploy the *interpretive, explanatory*, and *provocative* functions of humanistic research. Most of the questions we are confronted with in our globalized world cannot be solved without making use of interdisciplinary or transdisciplinary approaches. These, of course, are difficult to plan and resource, and they often cause a lot of headaches for university leaders as well as heads of funding institutions. Nevertheless, it is a necessity for all of us to try to provide preconditions for these ambitious endeavours to successfully cope with the complex realities of an increasingly multipolar and interconnected world in the 2020s and beyond.

Experience tells us that the integrative capacity of the humanities and social sciences can best be realized if the whole effort is conducted on a medium scale and driven by the complex problem itself. Only if the very problem to be tackled urges the researchers to combine their relevant expertise are they ultimately able to fully develop their integrative capacity and come up with surprising insights resulting in radically new perspectives and outstanding publications.[59]

To a large extent our academic institutions are still organized on a discipline by discipline basis. However, this institutional setting is itself the object of a value-laden critical analysis in that we ought to overcome some of the conceptual boundaries between disciplines in order to get their own value-foundations into view. This reflexive manoeuvre is essential for the task of coping with social complexity that includes the institutional repositioning of humanistic knowledge.[60]

One can distinguish between five different levels or attempts at integration when it comes to tackling at least some of the challenges we are confronted with:

1. The mere accumulation of methods and techniques is the most common form of combining different perspectives when looking at one and the same object. It is mainly multidisciplinary approaches that follow this path, and it usually allows all the researchers involved to address their preferred disciplinary communities. Often it is even required with respect to future careers of the junior researchers involved that they adhere to this self-sufficient disciplinary mode of a somewhat moderately integrated operation.

2. The integration of competencies from other disciplines is one of the most important ways of pursuing research questions of a global nature. For large parts of the humanities and social sciences (e.g. studies on modern China or India), it is even a prerequisite if one wants to produce sound insights concerning the respective region or topic, in particular when it comes to cross-cultural and comparative studies.

3. To develop different methods and disciplinary know-how in one and the same person is perhaps the most ambitious (and sometimes cumbersome) way of gaining the necessary degree of intimate knowledge about the object under study. If pursued with great competence and stamina, this approach can lead to outstanding results and globally acknowledged findings, represented in *opera magna* types of books that are translated into many other languages.

4. The interdisciplinary or transdisciplinary aggregation of competencies in a medium-scale research group is a complex endeavour, but if thematically as well as methodologically and organizationally integrated, it turns out to be the best way to proceed in most cases. The approach taken by the Danish National Research Foundation is perhaps the most successful one to date.

5. Problem-driven aggregations of skills are the most common approaches taken in large-scale projects and programmes. They are often confronted with enormous tensions: (1) between the heterogeneity of the phenomena to be studied and the aspiration towards methodological coherence throughout the project, (2) the tension between the often microscopic obsession with detail on the one hand, and striving for a comprehensive explanation on the other, sometimes even at the global level, (3) and last but not least the tendency of all involved to be self-sufficient in their disciplines, and at the same time a disposition to epistemic immodesty concerning knowledge claims with respect to the overarching goals. Cluster approaches taken by the humanities and social sciences are telling examples for these huge discrepancies between the objectives proposed and the everyday reality of the work done.

At the same time, it is essential for the humanities to draw on fundamental curiosity-driven 'blue sky' research, and thus avoid falling into the trap of becoming a 'service industry' for problem-solving in science and engineering. Instead, there is a clear need for them to autonomously develop their own, genuine research questions

TOWARDS A NEW ENLIGHTENMENT ■ MARKUS GABRIEL, CHRISTOPH HORN, ANNA KATSMAN, WILHELM KRULL, ANNA LUISA LIPPOLD, CORINE PELLUCHON, INGO VENZKE

45

which can prominently contribute to achieving social, cultural, or economic solutions. In our digitized and globalized world, with its multiple opportunities for networking and interacting with one another, it is indispensable that the humanities bring to the fore how much it helps us to grow our personalities and cultivate our virtues through these encounters. Ultimately, it is the other who helps me understand myself and my environment better than before. Such a contextualization of humanistic studies not only links the present to the past, but it also puts great hopes on the future.

5 Reconfiguring institutions – Towards a culture of creativity

Human behaviour and values (including central values like freedom, dignity, and wellbeing) are fundamentally tied to the structure of our social institutions. This is because human action and self-knowledge are necessarily shaped by social interactions that are patterned through institutions. As Hegel argued, individualist approaches or solutions to social problems are insufficient, because the rational freedom and wellbeing of individual lives are essentially bound up with the structure of our institutions. Humanistic inquiry must involve the critical study of the values held, both tacitly and explicitly, in our social institutions, examining their rational potential and deficits, and creating new institutions in line with our latest rational self-portraits.

An adequate institutional framework must be put in place for the humanities and social sciences to realize their full potential. Their potential is undermined not only when financial and material conditions are precarious, but also when they are squeezed into an instrumental logic and tied to technocratic descriptions of what problems are to be solved. We identify *four demands* for the institutional framework that enables a culture of creativity in the humanities and social sciences.[61]

1. Sufficient funding for research and education is a minimal condition. The demands of the humanities are far removed from those of the natural sciences, which require expensive technical and laboratory equipment. A wide funding gap between the humanities and experimental sciences – on average – is understandable. Patterns of defunding the humanities and further shifting resources to the natural and engineering sciences, however, shake the minimal conditions for the humanities to perform their crucial roles in society. Research must not be a weekend activity and the same number of teachers must not be left to cope with greater student numbers and bigger classes. Under these circumstances, research, education, and learning are bound to suffer.

2. The institutional framework must ensure a reliable, high-trust mode of core funding for teaching and research. That means placing more emphasis on the careful *ex ante assessment* and selection of both researchers and their projects, and less on ever tighter *ex post control* and reporting. For researchers and their projects, there is a fine line between risk-taking and measurable output. It is in the nature of creative research to ask questions whose answers are uncertain. It might lead to better understandings of the problem, rather than operational solutions.

3. This leads us to our third condition for an adequate institutional framework: What research should it reward? What counts as valuable? We have seen a tendency to submit the humanities and social sciences to problem descriptions as they arise from policy processes and managerial understandings of society. Their role is then reduced to the adjacent production of legitimacy. At its worst, and not unheard of, the humanities would be tied to promises of contributing to a country's gross domestic product (GDP).

Such an instrumentalization of the humanities would undercut their potential from the outset. For one thing, shifting understandings of what the problem is may be one of the humanities' main contribu-

TOWARDS A NEW ENLIGHTENMENT ■ MARKUS GABRIEL,
CHRISTOPH HORN, ANNA KATSMAN, WILHELM KRULL,
ANNA LUISA LIPPOLD, CORINE PELLUCHON, INGO VENZKE

47

tions and one of the most important drivers of societal change urgently needed in an ethics of transformation. It is necessary to crack dominant frames that confine problem descriptions and the scope of possible answers.[62] Humanities' role in this regard is even more necessary in view of current overlapping crises. It is necessary to conceptually slow down because the times are urgent, lest society remains stuck in the scheme that has been fuelling the crises. We see the role of the humanities in the practice of interpretation and understanding, and also in thought-provoking novel ways of understanding ourselves as part of society and nature. As for the vocation of research generally, the role cannot, at least not only, be to offer solutions and tell people what to do, but to provide 'inconvenient facts' that don't fit and challenge dominant frames of thinking.

4. To tap into their full potential, humanities' institutional framework must facilitate multidisciplinary and integrative work within and beyond their disciplinary boundaries. Critique remains powerless if it is not heard, and necessary provocations fail to appear across fragmented disciplines and related social spheres. The humanities need to open up towards the desires and anxieties of non-academic stakeholders while not subjecting their work to their demands. Stakeholders and their involvement must not be mistaken as a euphemism or fig leaf for the role and influence of private power. But isolating the humanities in view of that risk would be a wrong reaction, even part of the problem that we sketched at the outset. The institutional framework should enable multidisciplinary combinations while cherishing the proprium of each discipline and its distinct contributions.

Creating these new kinds of institutional ecosystems is in no way trivial. Nevertheless, there are some features which are more likely to foster creativity:[63] Most fundamentally, diversity, which must not be confused with mere heterogeneity. Building upon diversity in terms of gender, ethnicity, age, sexual orientation, etc. as a crucial precondition, diversity aims for an aggregation of different disciplines and sectors of society. To move from heterogeneity to diversity, active institutional curation is required. Curation includes the creation of ample opportunities for intense communication and interaction. If the institution is too small, the stimulus for extra-disciplinary orientation will be missing. If the facility is too large and heterogeneous, there will hardly be sufficient room for intense personal contacts and fertile exchanges.

With the need for thorough (self-)reflection in mind, establishing an atmosphere of sensitivity and mutual trust is vital. It has been shown to play an important role in increasing levels of empowerment, engagement, collaboration, and innovation. Enhancing an institutional governance that builds on and consistently demonstrates trusting and trust-enhancing behaviours is usually referred to as a high-trust culture. A high-trust culture ensures interactions on mutual respect, where promises and commitments are understood and fulfilled, as well as the forming of meaningful and supportive relationships.

Each discipline has its own traditions, theories, methods, and focuses, which may eventually cause obstacles to discussions even within a single discipline. The same is true for different sectors. As a result, joint interdisciplinary and intersectoral work may occasionally resemble speaking different professional languages. In order to cooperatively move towards new pathways for the future, interdisciplinary discussions require sustainable modes of translation. For at least a decade, there has been a growing number of programmes (not only in the humanities and social sciences), which aim to educate scholars who are familiar with more than one discipline and to foster interdisciplinarity within one person. This kind of translation may be seen as facilitating the connectivity of disciplines to one another.

By putting these features at the heart of building or reshaping institutions of the humanities and social sciences, there is a chance not only to discover any new pathways but to discover those that reach society by creating a sense of ownership among and between all parties involved.

TOWARDS A NEW ENLIGHTENMENT ■ MARKUS GABRIEL,
CHRISTOPH HORN, ANNA KATSMAN, WILHELM KRULL,
ANNA LUISA LIPPOLD, CORINE PELLUCHON, INGO VENZKE

49

6 Towards a New Enlightenment

In their contributions towards a sustainable future, the humanities and social sciences should not limit themselves to criticizing the shortcomings and social pathologies of the current development model. They can connect past, present, and future by bringing their diverse methods to bear on issues of global social concern. In this way, they do not merely describe or analytically criticize modern social formations but can actively and creatively shape them. In this way, they can orient themselves in light of a conception of a desirable future, an orientation designed to overcome the apocalyptic deadlock which currently constrains our social imaginaries for an open and potentially better future.

In today's critical situation, there is a widespread call for a New Enlightenment no longer limited to prolonging the projects of the 17th and 18th century European Enlightenment. One of the distinctive features of a New Enlightenment is that it will have worked through the justified critique of the false universals and dialectics of the European Enlightenment which resulted in the modern decoupling of technoscientific progress from notions of human flourishing and moral progress.

Constantly renewing the link between theory and practice thanks to the critical reflection that indicates which value representations, mindsets, and social practices ought to be rejected and exceeded characterizes the Enlightenment ethos.[64] It also explains that Enlightenment is always associated with a project of individual and collective emancipation and a critical use of our capacities of imagination.[65]

Key principles
Four key principles constitute the Enlightenment: The defence of autonomy, a society based on freedom and equality, equality among human beings, and the defence of philosophical-scientific rationality.

The central idea behind the defence of autonomy is that the future is uncertain, and that humanity can take its destiny into its own

THE NEW
INSTITUTE

hands through reflexive, critical activity. Instead of basing society on heteronomy, in particular on religion and essentialist worldviews that justify the enslavement of a part of humanity and the maintenance of hierarchies, the Enlightenment promotes an ideal of individual and collective emancipation.

This way of making autonomy the key to emancipation also explains the desire to establish a society based on freedom and equality, and not on heteronomous and hierarchical order. This is the second principle that characterizes the Enlightenment and proves that it is always connected with a political project.

This project, which takes the form of democracy or republicanism, goes hand in hand with the affirmation of equality among human beings. This is the third principle of the Enlightenment. It is concretized in the defence of human rights. However, the content of these principles is renewed over time. Their defence sometimes requires that the foundations of the past Enlightenment are critically examined.

For example, whereas the first generation of human rights pertains to the political sphere, the second generation focuses on social and economic conditions. Moreover, if the inclusive dynamic of today's liberal democracies is to show fidelity to the principle of equality, it is necessary for minorities to question the hegemonic universalism and eurocentrism of the past Enlightenment in order to be recognized as full citizens. In the same way, the 2015 Universal Declaration of Human Rights supplements the declaration of human rights while making the protection of the natural and cultural heritage of humanity as well as the concern not to mortgage the living conditions of future generations new imperatives limiting the rights of individuals.

Not only do freedom, dignity, and peace between peoples depend on the preservation of the conditions of life on earth, but, in addition, it is necessary to go beyond the atomistic and abstract foundation of the past Enlightenment in order to take into account the materiality of our existence and our dependence on nature and on others, human and other than human.[66]

The fourth main principle of the Enlightenment defends philosophical-scientific rationality in order to fight against superstition and mythology. Reason is the privileged instrument of emancipation. It overcomes prejudices and justifies the cessation of outdated, unfair, and even violent practices.

TOWARDS A NEW ENLIGHTENMENT ■ MARKUS GABRIEL, CHRISTOPH HORN, ANNA KATSMAN, WILHELM KRULL, ANNA LUISA LIPPOLD, CORINE PELLUCHON, INGO VENZKE

51

Key challenges

These four principles are rejected by the Anti-Enlightenment, whose contempt for human rights and hatred of reason serve the project of establishing a hierarchical and heteronomous society.[67] The Anti-Enlightenment opposes nationalism against human rights and rejects the idea of the unity of the human race and cosmopolitanism by proclaiming that particular communities, based on tradition or even ethnicity, are incompatible. It thus justifies the subjugation of one nation by another and of some human beings by others.

This conflict between the Enlightenment and Anti-Enlightenment is particularly relevant at a time when we are witnessing the awakening of nationalisms, the return of fanaticism and theocratic claims, and at a time when there is war in Europe, after the invasion of Ukraine by Russia. The distrust of channels of knowledge, i.e. the sciences, and the discrediting of democratic institutions, which are accused of being incapable of remedying market deregulation and reducing inequalities, also underlines the importance of referring to the Enlightenment. However, it is not enough to simply apply these principles to the current situation. Supplementation is required, as described above with human rights.

In general, the former Enlightenment anthropology needs to be supplemented with the taking into account of our earthly condition and vulnerability. This leads to a reconfiguration of autonomy in light of our dependence on nature and other beings. Moreover, this Enlightenment is new because of the epistemological and technological ruptures existing between the eighteenth century and today, but also and above all because it is born after the eclipse of the Enlightenment due to the tragedies of the 20th century and postmodern critiques.

Daring to speak of Enlightenment today requires being aware of the blind spots and errors of the past Enlightenment.[68] However, postmodernists must not be confused with the Anti-Enlightenment: Far from rejecting the Enlightenment project of emancipation and its ideal of justice, feminists and post-colonialists rightly show that it has been unable to keep its promises of a more inclusive society. Their critiques should be taken seriously: the past Enlightenment has defended a false universalism by using so-called universal principles to hide the desire to impose a hegemonic lifestyle on other cultures.

THE NEW
INSTITUTE

Not only must the reversal of rationality into irrationality and barbarism be explained, but we must also be aware of the tendency of all universalisms to become hegemonic and blind to differences. It is imperative to create the conditions for a true dialogue with other cultures. Lastly, the New Enlightenment must aim at responding to current ecological and economic challenges, which are largely the consequence of a model of development based on the unlimited exploitation of nature, of other living beings and of some human beings by others. The New Enlightenment must offer pathways towards promoting a fairer and ecologically sustainable model of development while exploring and elaborating options to recouple economic prosperity and humanistic goals, and even how to overcome capitalism.

These are the three main challenges of the New Enlightenment. Its ability to meet these challenges is the condition of its relevance. This goal also stresses the humanities as specific and irreplaceable in today's society. If the humanities can defend this project of a New Enlightenment and be future-oriented by offering some keys to get us out of the current impasse, it is because they seek to explain the link between the political, ecological, technological, and geopolitical challenges mentioned above. In spite of a diversity of approaches and perspectives, or rather thanks to them, it is actually possible to connect around a common project, which could open up a horizon of hope. In order to justify this affirmation, we have to answer some questions.

Open questions guiding the way forward

The first question concerns the diagnosis or the genealogy of nihilism. Which amputation of reason explains the deviation of rationalism and this reversal of progress into regression that gave birth to phenomena like totalitarianism, Nazism, capitalism, and the destruction of the planet? Do these phenomena have a common root? Why didn't the past Enlightenment preserve us from such a destructive dialectic?

The second question concerns our capacity to promote a non-hegemonic rationalism. This implies a return to the notion of lateral universalism, which not only involves taking responsibility for the colonialism of the past Enlightenment but requires a culture of difference in the sense that Derrida gives to this term, namely, thinking

TOWARDS A NEW ENLIGHTENMENT ■ MARKUS GABRIEL,
CHRISTOPH HORN, ANNA KATSMAN, WILHELM KRULL,
ANNA LUISA LIPPOLD, CORINE PELLUCHON, INGO VENZKE

53

of the way other cultures challenge and displace us.[69] How is it possible to achieve this goal?

To answer the first question, it is necessary to critically examine modern and contemporary rationalism. An inquiry into rationality that aims at explaining the reversal of progress into regression leads to denouncing instrumental reason which is characterized by the fact that the latter is reduced to calculation and does not enable us to distinguish between right and wrong. However, this diagnosis we find in Adorno and Horkheimer does not suffice. We also have to question the dualism of nature and culture that permeates the West. This dualism and radical separation between humans and other living beings engenders a violent humanism founded on the oblivion of our condition as living beings. It is largely responsible, as Claude Lévi-Strauss says, for the discriminations and tragedies of the 20th century.[70]

Because such dualism is specific to our civilization, the New Enlightenment is inseparable from an anthropological revolution that entails the questioning of whole sections of our education. It calls for reconciliation with our finitude and our carnal and earthly condition. Beyond this existential and anthropological dimension, which refers to the way humans perceive their place in nature, it is also important to insist on the role of the social and economic structures that shape our psyche and explain our behaviour with regard to others, both human and non-human. For this, it is helpful to think in terms of the notion of a 'scheme' and specifically of a scheme of domination (Pelluchon, 2021a: 98–99): A scheme is the set of conscious and unconscious representations that determine our social, economic, and political choices. It is a matrix or a dynamic device that organizes modes of production, assigns a value to certain activities and objects, and intrudes into people's minds. To speak of the scheme of a society is to say that we are dealing with a mental map which imposes a development model. Our society is governed by the scheme of domination, which is a threefold domination, as Adorno and Horkheimer have said: over others, over external nature, and over our internal nature. This is to say, it is linked to the repression of our nature or carnal condition. The scheme of domination implies a predatory relationship with nature, the commodification of living beings (including oneself), constant competition, and the obsession with mastery and external control.

It transforms husbandry, work, politics, and even human relationships into a kind of war.

Nowadays, the scheme of domination takes the socio-economic form of neoliberal capitalism, which is an organization structured around the rule of profit and the subordination of all activities to the economy narrowly construed. However, to speak of a scheme avoids limiting ourselves to denouncing capitalism without understanding the reasons it is still victorious despite its multiple perverse effects, which are at once environmental, sanitary, social, and political. The notion of the scheme also allows us to say that, if it alienates us, we have nevertheless instituted it. We can dispose of what we have instituted.

Many scholars would like to bring humanistic insight to the table of public deliberation concerning the very shape of economic activity.[71] In the absence of a deep shift in one's mindset, it is often wishful thinking. On the contrary, when ecology defined as the rationality (*logos*) of our inhabitation of the earth (*oikos*) and understood in its environmental, social, and anthropological or existential dimension, it has an emancipatory force: It can dispense with the scheme of domination because it requires that we overcome a narrow anthropocentrism and put into question the dualism between nature and culture. This existential transformation leads to acknowledgement of the value of each being and to making room for other beings. Thus, ecology implies the reconciliation of nature and civilization both at the individual level of representations and lifestyles and at the collective level of structural transformations linked to the reorientation of economy and changes in production modes.

As ecology means taking into account our interdependence and the community of vulnerability that unifies all living beings, it modifies our mindsets and mental maps from top to bottom. It also generates powerful affects like wonder, compassion, gratitude, and the desire to cooperate. This emancipatory force explains why ecology is the translation, on the social, economic, and political level, of the scheme of consideration which makes the value of each being and the preservation of the common world the two goals from which to guide economic, technological, and political choices. The New Enlightenment is therefore inseparable from a renewed conception of the human being whose freedom and dependence on others and nature are equally acknowledged. Can this humanism be suspected

TOWARDS A NEW ENLIGHTENMENT ■ MARKUS GABRIEL, CHRISTOPH HORN, ANNA KATSMAN, WILHELM KRULL, ANNA LUISA LIPPOLD, CORINE PELLUCHON, INGO VENZKE

55

of excluding other cultures and of re-entrenching the domination of certain nations over others, of men over women, of humans over animals? How can we think of a common project that rests on universalizable foundations while welcoming difference and without making the recognition of diversity a mere word or alibi?

To answer this second set of questions, we have to acknowledge that the former humanism was based on elitist criteria, chosen in reference to a model set up as a norm. On the contrary, the humanism characteristic of the New Enlightenment as well as its insistence on the relational dimension of the human being and on our embodiment, is inclusive: although society and culture constitute large parts of our identity, all beings have a body, we need air, water, food. The degradation of nature represents a global and universal threat.

Reality is not an apprehension from above dictated by an overarching reason claiming to have a total vision of things. Nonetheless, it is possible to describe phenomena in an objective way, albeit partial, as we see in the method of phenomenology. The plurality of approaches is essential to the New Enlightenment. It is an unfinished process and is perspectival. Moreover, the awareness of the partial character of its approach and of the blind spots that dictate its perspective, as well as the memory of the faults committed in the name of an arrogant rationalism, must make possible a true dialogue between cultures. It is not a question of simply welcoming other cultures in order to avoid the accusation of Eurocentrism. The point to understand, as Derrida stresses when speaking of Europe, is that the Enlightenment lives through its difference. It actually lives through this difference with itself, through this gap and its self-critique. This is not to be confused with saying that a culture does not have an identity. It means that its characteristic, in particular when it defends an ideal of emancipation, is 'to be able to say "me" or "we"; to be able to take the form of a subject only in the non-identity to itself... in the difference *with itself [avec soi]*' (Derrida, 1992, 9–10, original emphasis).

Under these conditions, it is possible to achieve a balance between universalism and historicity which is the condition for an intercultural dialogue that allows us to avoid two impasses: cultural particularism and the impossible communication between peoples, on the one hand, and Eurocentrism and cultural colonialism on the other.[72] The stakes are considerable: it is true that the supporters of any hegemonic universalism seek to impose a particular way of life to the detriment of others, but the supporters of relativism and cultural particularism who deny any common horizon represent another dead end, since they can generate hostility between peoples. Moreover, they leave the way open to the Anti-Enlightenment as well as to those who want to defend the status quo and business as usual instead of achieving ecological transition.

The paradigm of this intercultural hermeneutic or of this balance between universalism and historicity is translation.[73] Just as humanity is both one and plural, things can be said in other ways and thus be different each time. Translation actually forces one to find in one's own language an equivalent of what is said in another idiom. In so doing, the translator thinks between languages, opening up to another way of mapping reality and rediscovering at the same time their own language. Things can be put differently, whether in another language or even by a reformulation in one's own language. We can thereby be enriched by a real dialogue with other cultures that can enlighten us, in particular on questions relating to our relationship with death, nature, and with other living beings.

7 Suggestions for the way ahead

It is time to bring the full range of humanistic and social-scientific knowledge to bear on the urgent issues of our time in an institutional context of large-scale cooperation. For this, we need a new 'spirit of trust', as Brandom (2019) calls it in his book with the same title, which allows us to rethink the global social formations within which human becoming takes place in the 21st century.

The approach of the New Enlightenment project re-couples value perspectives with large-scale cooperation between different sectors of society and hence may restore the link between theory and practice. It invites a number of contextual and trans-sectoral research endeavours, including the following:

TOWARDS A NEW ENLIGHTENMENT ■ MARKUS GABRIEL,
CHRISTOPH HORN, ANNA KATSMAN, WILHELM KRULL,
ANNA LUISA LIPPOLD, CORINE PELLUCHON, INGO VENZKE

57

Coping with complexity

Social complexity involves the first-person perspective. Subjective experience is an indispensable dimension of social formations. Systemic thinking presupposes recognition of the socio-economic, historical situatedness of human agency in context. Thus, the humanities and social sciences are ideally suited to (i) describe the development of social complexity and to (ii) reshape the societal scheme within which sensemaking takes place. Thereby they contribute normative guidelines to desirable change by investigating the complex entanglement of different normative spheres from the individual to the collective level and vice versa. Social complexity has a circular or feedback loop structure. At the core of this structure is human becoming that both influences and is influenced by its integration into natural and social conditions.

The humanities and social sciences can develop tools for coping with complexity. They can orient themselves towards the future by designing realistic utopias and models for positive social change which respect the irreducible complexity and contingency of our individual and collective value orientation. For this reason, they are precisely not in the business of reducing complexity in order to generate quick, but unsustainable solutions. Shifting the solution space towards sustainable modes of ethical transformation consists in creating a culture of creativity that can appreciate the need to come to terms with the multiple facets of complex phenomena.

Complexity does not undermine decision-making; it rather conditions its successful realization. This crucial fact of the human condition is made visible by the various disciplines of the human and social sciences that allow us to identify possible and realizable future goals so as to then identify appropriate means for socially desirable goals.

Interdisciplinary integration of the humanities and social sciences strives for trans-sectoral cooperation. While genuine multi-perspectivity transcends the boundaries of academic knowledge-acquisition, it ought to integrate the humanities and social sciences and bring their knowledge to the table of a future-oriented mode of transformation. The critical tools of the humanities thereby contribute to positive design by adding knowledge of value representation and academically rigorous value-judgements to the large-scale New Enlightenment project of shaping novel visions of the good on a level with the global challenges of the 21st century.

THE NEW
INSTITUTE

Welcoming otherness

False universalism, dismissive of difference and otherness, suppresses crucial sources of knowledge by those individuals and collectives that do not fit under its hegemonic concepts. The universality of the New Enlightenment, by contrast, is not static, but involves continuous decolonization and dynamic universalization. Shared humanity is a task and a process of ongoing making and remaking, a task that requires both trust and creativity. For this, a posture of welcoming otherness, compassion, empathy, and listening to others, is required. This means not knowing ahead of time what others will bring, being radically challenged and possibly uprooted, and remaining in a stance of openness in the name of building togetherness. While welcoming otherness is not without tension and difficulty, it does not mean that there are not true universals we share in virtue of who we are as humans. The 'we' is both constructed and denied, again and again, in the ongoing process of making sense in common, on the basis of both a shared humanity and diverse knowledge perspectives. This presupposes large-scale cooperation across sectors, including politics, business, the arts, media, and public discourse, which constitutes the self-understanding of a given social formation.

The New Enlightenment brings together diverse knowledges across sectors, cultures, and problem spaces. There is much to learn from building perspectives across cultures on a wide array of issues. What are various ways that human beings conceive of the relationship between humankind and the natural world? Transcultural, value-rich perspectives on soil, water, landscapes, and animals help with creatively imagining alternative structures of governance and ownership, ones hospitable to both human and planetary wellbeing. Shifting mental maps towards greater social cohesion in virtue of shared ends and pursuits can be sparked by examining different architectures and narratives through which cultures balance the authority of the individual with the social.

Ecologizing systemically

In the face of climate change and environmental degradation – crises driven by a dominating rationality that decouples technological progress from ethics – society, politics, and the economy are to be ecologized. The project of ecologizing must be systematic, cut across many sectors of society, and bring together different actors. For this

TOWARDS A NEW ENLIGHTENMENT ■ MARKUS GABRIEL,
CHRISTOPH HORN, ANNA KATSMAN, WILHELM KRULL,
ANNA LUISA LIPPOLD, CORINE PELLUCHON, INGO VENZKE

59

to succeed, it is indispensable to work from a truly ecological perspective, one that sees humans as engaging in activities of niche construction alongside other living beings within interdependent ecosystems. Only with such a perspective will the socio-economic, political transformation towards a sustainable way of life to be true to its name.

One of the main challenges today is how to fill the gap between theory and practice; many know what needs to be done, yet action stalls year after year. This calls for value-based, sociological investigation into successful strategies for shifting production and consumption patterns at both individual and institutional levels. Research is required to understand the practices and mindsets that motivate and enable individuals, singularly and collectively, to overcome unsustainable production and consumption patterns. Investigation into existing alternative practices of ecologically minded living, such as transition towns and cooperatives, can inspire new approaches. What values undergird the practices there? What binds people to these values and to one another? What are their conditions of success and failure? What are the possibilities of scalability, and what resources might be helpful for such scalability? Since new practices and mental schemes require new value representations, creative arts and literature are crucial contributors to building stories, narratives, songs, and cosmologies that see the human embedded within nature.

Reconfiguring public health

The past decades have witnessed a dramatic increase in the privatization of healthcare markets, increasing intermediaries and middlemen between doctors and patients, and the involvement of multinational companies. Healthcare has become more bureaucratized, politicized, privatized, and differentially accessible based on factors like class, race, and nation. In the wake of the Covid-19 pandemic, we see how fragile and interdependent our local, national, and global healthcare systems are. The pandemic demands new ways of thinking about what is in the public interest. The commercialization of health must be analysed and criticized. What kind of good is health? What does it mean to be healthy? What follows for society when health is considered a public good, or, indeed, a human right? How much should society spend in the health sector?

THE NEW
INSTITUTE

A new value-based approach requires that we rethink the objectives of a new health system, rediscovering health as a public good after a long phase of neoliberalism capitalizing on public health issues. A healthcare system responsive to the human condition begins with the recognition that we are finite, vulnerable beings who depend on one another's care. Which national healthcare systems and global health architecture improve access and diversify quality options for people? How must future local and global health institutions be structured to ensure the necessary level of collective action and rapid response for future health crises?

Reconciling technology and culture

The tremendous growth of technical knowledge has brought advancements in critical infrastructure, education, communication, commerce, transportation, food production, health, and has raised living standards across the world. AI is facilitating dramatic shifts in education, especially during the Covid-19 pandemic, where personalized learning has come even more to the fore. At the same time, the technologically facilitated domination and exploitation of nature is a major driver of climate change and has contributed to the rise of echo chambers, political polarization, and social fragmentation in our media networks. AI comes with the risks of authoritarian surveillance and control, endangering the values of individual liberty and human rights, and exacerbating inequality within and across countries as monopolies over data grow.

Technologies can only facilitate freedom and flourishing if they are created and situated within ethical horizons of thinking about values and outcomes. Research is required to elaborate the values and normative foundations that undergird global standards with regard to the sustainability as well as the responsible development and use of AI infrastructure. Successful adoption of AI will drive economies, reshape societies, and determine which countries set the rules for the coming century.

TOWARDS A NEW ENLIGHTENMENT ■ MARKUS GABRIEL,
CHRISTOPH HORN, ANNA KATSMAN, WILHELM KRULL,
ANNA LUISA LIPPOLD, CORINE PELLUCHON, INGO VENZKE

61

Summary

Humanity is faced with fundamental challenges and, taking re-search-based scenarios seriously, it will continue to be confronted with a host of global, interwoven, and increasingly complex crises. As a result of this seemingly ever-increasing dynamic, uncertainty and urgency seem to dominate our future. Considering the possibil-ity to secure the uncertain and to postpone the pressing is no longer an option. Instead, we suggest making a case for future-oriented hu-manities, which may provide a foundation for a New Enlightenment carried by an interdisciplinary, trans-sectoral collectivity. In this re-spect, we propose the following:

1. The overarching goal must be to recouple the human-ities with disciplines and sectors that have traditionally defined the direction and scope of tools used to cope with diverse challenges.
2. The humanities should strive for providing the much-needed compass called 'becoming human in the 21st century', which may structure, shift, and align all current and future steps towards individual, collective, and institutional change.
3. Facing the need to build bridges between disciplines and sectors, cultures and continents, as well as past, present, and future, the humanities must make use of their integrative capacity.
4. To contribute to the range of options for a constructive, innovative, and positive future, the humanities can and should use methods which go beyond criticism and critique, including the development of programmes that moderate and successfully recombine competencies from different disciplines and sectors.
5. A fundamentally revised idea of institution-building that facilitates creative collaboration is required to realize the humanities' full potential.

THE NEW
INSTITUTE

6. A New Enlightenment as a project which essentially aims to overcome various schemes of domination may be carried by a diverse, yet – and perhaps even thereby – united range of actors.
7. Joint endeavours may include: The creation of a new approach to coping with complexity, the exploration of new perspectives for a dynamic process of universalizing that we can all share as human beings, the inquiry into new practices that systematically place environmental matters at the core, and the investigation of new ways of thinking about what is in the public interest and how to strengthen resilience in this regard.

All in all, this Discussion Paper is a plea for a fundamental reorientation of the humanities as well as a reorientation of the public discourse calling the humanities and social sciences to action.[74] But more importantly, it is an invitation to embark upon a journey with us towards creating the conceptual foundations of a New Enlightenment.

Notes

[1]   See Lima de Miranda and Snower (2020) and Gabriel (2020a).

[2]   See Madsbjerg (2017) and Russell (2019).

[3]   See also Nakajima (2021).

[4]   See also Gabriel (2018).

[5]   See Eshel (2019).

[6]   See Spivak (2007).

[7]   See e.g. Fricker (2007) and Kohn (2013).

[8]   See Ober (2010).

[9]   See e.g. Annas (1993).

[10]   See Zeuske (2018), as a paradigm for humanistic, value-driven scrutiny.

[11]   See Sen (1977).

[12]   See Dilthey (1992).

[13]   See Weber (1988).

[14]   See Habermas (2019a, 2019b, 2015).

[15]   Most recently see Dreyfus and Taylor (2015) and the impressive account of the humanities in Habermas (2019a, 2019b).

[16]   On this notion within the context of a theory of the humanities and social sciences see Gabriel (2020b).

[17]   See Bal (2002).

[18]   See Weber (1904).

[19]   See Weber (1918).

[20]   See Putnam (1981) and Putnam (2004).

[21]   Honneth (1995: 269).

[22]   See Daston and Galison (2007).

[23]   See Srinivasan (2019).

[24]   See Descola (2014) and Latour (2009).

[25]   See Kaup (2021) and Danowski and Viveiros de Castro (2016).

[26]   Such as the classic Chakrabarty (2007) and Spivak (1999).

[27]   See Forst (2020).

THE NEW
INSTITUTE

[28]   See Ophir (2005).

[29]   See the history of universalism in Zhao (2021).

[30]   See Ricœur (2008).

[31]   See Kennedy (2014).

[32]   See Kraut (2018).

[33]   See the new book series Reality and Hermeneutics (Gabriel et al. 2022). A paradigmatic work in this style is Jessica Riskin's *The Restless Clock*, which shows with great historical detail how the digital transformation rests on a theological prehistory of voiding the machine world and then the microbiological level from the idea of meaningful agency (Riskin 2016, see also Cobb 2020). This has in turn produced conditions of a machine age where human decision-making is obscured by complex automated processes to such an extent that specialists from the technological field are asking for a recoupling of economics, machine learning, and the humanities in order to create anthropogenic digital systems that promote our well-being, see Russell (2019).

[34]   See Eco (1990) and Gumbrecht (2004a).

[35]   See Scanlon (2000).

[36]   See Ricœur (1992) and Pelluchon (2021a).

[37]   See Shafer-Landau (2003), Railton (2003) Gabriel (2020a), and Scanlon (2014). The PhilPapers surveys consistently show that most professional philosophers (most recent survey: 56.4% versus 27.7% who endorse the opposite sort of view, moral anti-realism) accept or lean towards moral realism. https://philpapers.org/surveys/results.pl. Of course, this does not prove that they are right. However, we should neglect the fact that the discipline of metaethics is certainly not predominantly anti-realist, let alone relativist, nihilist, or sceptical about objective moral value, as many people outside of the field might expect.

[38]   See Pelluchon (2022).

[39]   On this concept see Forst and Günther (2021).

[40]   See Korsgaard (1996, 2008, 2009).

[41]   See Pelluchon (2020).

[42]   See Pelluchon (2019).

[43]   See Merleau-Ponty (1960, 1983) and Pelluchon (2021a).

[44]   See Merleau-Ponty (1960, 1983).

TOWARDS A NEW ENLIGHTENMENT ■ MARKUS GABRIEL, CHRISTOPH HORN, ANNA KATSMAN, WILHELM KRULL, ANNA LUISA LIPPOLD, CORINE PELLUCHON, INGO VENZKE

65

45   See Horkheimer (2013).

46   See Furet (2000).

47   See Lyotard (1984).

48   See Parfit (2011), Leiter (2010, 2013).

49   See Luhrmann (2020).

50   See Beckert (2016) and Beckert and Bronk (2018).

51   See Stanley (2016).

52   See Gabriel (2018, 2020b).

53   See Ferraris (2012) and most recently Ferraris (2021).

54   See Bogdandy (2022).

55   See Venzke (2022).

56   See Srinivasan (2019).

57   See Krull (2000, 2011).

58   As cited in Krull (2014).

59   See Krull (2015).

60   See Gordon (2006).

61   See for this section Krull (2009, 2012).

62   See Venzke (2016).

63   For the following paragraphs: see Krull (2009, 2014, 2015).

64   See Foucault (1984c).

65   See Garces (2019).

66   See Pelluchon (2019, 2021a, 2021b).

67   See Sternhell (2009).

68   See Garces (2019), Gabriel and Nakajima (2020).

69   See Derrida (1992).

70   See Lévi-Strauss (2004).

71   See Frevert (2020) and Frevert et al. (2019).

72   See Ricœur (1992).

73   See Ricœur (1992).

74   For a more nuanced view on the social sciences see Mulgan (2021, 2022).

THE NEW
INSTITUTE

References

Anderson, Benedict (2016): *Imagined Communities: Reflections on the Origin and Spread of Nationalism*, Revised Edition, London: Verso, ISBN: 9781784786755

Annas, Julia (1993): *The Morality of Happiness*, 1st Edition, Oxford: Oxford University Press, ISBN: 9780195079999

Bal, Mieke (2002): *Traveling Concepts in the Humanities*, 1st Edition, Toronto: University of Toronto Press, ISBN: 9780802084101

Beckert, Jens (2016): *Imagined Futures: Fictional Expectations and Capitalist Dynamics*, 1st Edition, Cambridge, MA: Harvard University Press, ISBN: 9780674088825

Beckert, Jens and Bronk, Richard (2018): *Uncertain Futures: Imaginaries, Narratives, and Calculation in the Economy*, 1st Edition, Oxford: Oxford University Press, ISBN: 9780198820802

Bevir, Mark (1994): Objectivity in History, *History and Theory*, 33(3), 328–344 [online], https://escholarship.org/uc/item/5h42j7jn

Bogdandy, Armin von (2022): *Der Strukturwandel des Öffentlichen Rechts: Entstehung und Demokratisierung der Europäischen Gesellschaft*, 1st Edition, Berlin: Suhrkamp Verlag, ISBN: 9783518299562

Brandom, Robert B. (2019): *A Spirit of Trust: A Reading of Hegel's Phenomenology*, 1st Edition, Cambridge, MA: Harvard University Press, ISBN: 9780674976818

Chakrabarty, Dipesh (2007): *Provincializing Europe: Postcolonial Thought and Historical Differences*, New Edition, Princeton, NJ: Princeton University Press, ISBN: 9780691130019

Cobb, Matthew (2020): *The Idea of the Brain: A History*, 1st Edition, London: Profile Books, ISBN: 9781781255896

Cover, Robert (1983): Nomos and Narrative, *Harvard Law Review*, 97(4), https://heinonline.org/HOL/LandingPage?handle=hein.journals/hlr97&div=13&id=&page=

Danowski, Déborah and Viveros de Castro, Eduardo (2016): *The Ends of the World*, 1st Edition, Cambridge: Polity, ISBN: 9781509503988

Daston, Lorraine and Galison, Peter (2007): *Objectivity*, 5th Edition, Princeton, NJ: Princeton University Press, ISBN: 978-1-890951-79-5

TOWARDS A NEW ENLIGHTENMENT ■ MARKUS GABRIEL,
CHRISTOPH HORN, ANNA KATSMAN, WILHELM KRULL,
ANNA LUISA LIPPOLD, CORINE PELLUCHON, INGO VENZKE

67

Derrida, Jacques (1992): *The Other Heading: Reflections on Today's Europe*, originally published in French as (1991) *L'autre Cap, Les Editions de Minuit*, trans. Pascale-Anne Brault and Michael B. Naas, Bloomington, IN: Indiana University Press, ANSI Z39.48-1984

Descola, Philippe (2014): *Beyond Nature and Culture*, New Edition, Chicago, IL: University of Chicago Press, ISBN: 9780226212364

Dewey, John (1954): *The Public and Its Problems*, New Edition, Athens, OH: Swallow Press, ISBN: 9780804002547

Dilthey, Wilhelm (1992): *Gesammelte Werke Band 7: Der Aufbau der geschichtlichen Welt der Geisteswissenschaften*, 1st Edition, Göttingen: Vandenhoeck & Ruprecht, ISBN: 9783525303085

Dreyfus, Hubert and Taylor, Charles (2015): *Retrieving Realism*, 1st Edition, Cambridge, MA: Harvard University Press, ISBN: 97806 74967519

Eco, Umberto (1990): *The Limits of Interpretation.* 1st Edition, Bloomington, IN: Indiana University Press, ISBN: 9780253318527

Eshel, Amir (2019): *Poetic Thinking Today*, 1st Edition, Stanford, CA: Stanford University Press, ISBN: 9781503608870

Ferraris, Maurizio (2012): *Documentality: Why It Is Necessary to Leave Traces*, 1st Edition, Bronx, NY: Fordham University Press, ISBN: 9780823249688

Ferraris, Maurizio (2021): *Documanità: Filosofia del mondo nuovo.* 1st Edition, Bari: I Robinson / Letture, ISBN: 9788858134115

Forst, Rainer (2020): A Critical Theory of Transnational (In-)Justice: Realistic in the Right Way, in: Brooks, Thom (2020): *The Oxford Handbook of Global Justice*, 1st Edition, Oxford: Oxford University Press, ISBN: 9780198714354

Forst, Rainer and Günther, Klaus (2021): *Normative Ordnung*, 1st Edition, Berlin: Suhrkamp Verlag, ISBN: 9783518299425

Forum Humanum (2021, 25 October): *On Not Thinking Straight: Stupidity, Trust and the Ethics of Vaccine Hesitancy in the Anthropocene* [Video], https://www.forum-humanum.org/was-wir-tun/mediathek/on-not-thinking-straight.html

Foucault, Michel (1984): What Is Enlightenment?, in: Rabinow, Paul (1991): *The Foucault Reader: An Introduction to Foucault's Thought*, New Edition, London: Penguin Books, ISBN: 9780140124866

Frevert, Ute (2020): *Kapitalismus, Märkte und Moral*, München: dtv, ISBN: 9783423349833

Frevert, Ute; Fontaine, Laurence; Suter Mischa; Danilina, Anna; E
Björn; Rohringer, Thomas; Kreis, Reinhild; and Großmann,
(2019): *Moral Economies*, 1st Edition, Göttingen: Vandenhoed
Ruprecht, ISBN: 9783525364260

Fricker, Miranda (2007): *Epistemic Injustice: Power and the Ethi
Knowing*, 1st Edition, Oxford: Oxford University Press, ISBN: 9
198237907

Fukuyama, Francis (1989): The End of History?, *The National Inter
16, 3–18 [online], https://www.jstor.org/stable/24027184

Furet, Francois (2000): *The Passing of an Illusion: The Idea of Com
nism in the Twentieth Century*, New Edition, Chicago, IL: Univers
of Chicago Press, ISBN: 9780226273419

Gabriel, Markus (2018): *Neo-Existentialism*, 1st Edition, Cambridg
Polity, ISBN: 9781509532476

Gabriel, Markus (2020a): *Moralischer Fortschritt in Dunklen Zeite
Universale Werte für das 21. Jahrhundert*, 5th Edition, Berlin: Ullste
Verlag, ISBN: 9783550081941 (English, see Gabriel, forthcomi
December 2022)

Gabriel, Markus (2020b): *Fiktionen*, 1st Edition, Berlin: Suhrkamp Ve
lag, ISBN: 9783518587485

Gabriel, Markus (2021): Could a Robot Be Conscious? Some Lesso
from Philosophy, in: von Braun, Joachim; Archer, Margaret, S.; R
ichberg, Gregory, M. and Sánchez Sorondo, Marcelo (2021): *R
botics, AI and Humanity*, 1st Edition, Cham, Switzerland: Springe
ISBN: 9783030541729

Gabriel, Markus (2022, forthcoming): *Moral Progress in Dark Times*, 1s
Edition, Cambridge: Polity

Gabriel, Markus and Nakajima, Takahiro (2020): 全体主義の克服
Tokyo: 集英社, ISBN: 9784087211320

Gabriel, Markus; Gymnich, Marion; Keiling, Tobias and Münch, Birgit
U. (2022): *Reality and Hermeneutics*, Tübingen: Mohr Siebeck

Garces, Marina (2019): *Neue Radikale Aufklärung*, 1st Edition, Vienna:
Turia + Kant, ISBN: 9783851329384

Gordon, Lewis R. (2006): *Disciplinary Decadence: Living Thought in Trying Times*, 1st Edition, London: Routledge, ISBN: 9781594512568

Gumbrecht, Hans U. (2004a): *Production of Presence: What Meaning
Cannot Convey*, 1st Edition, Stanford, CA: Stanford University Press,
ISBN: 9780804749169

TOWARDS A NEW ENLIGHTENMENT ▪ MARKUS GABRIEL,
CHRISTOPH HORN, ANNA KATSMAN, WILHELM KRULL,
ANNA LUISA LIPPOLD, CORINE PELLUCHON, INGO VENZKE

69

Gumbrecht, Hans, U. (2004b): The Task of Humanities Today, in: Casado Jensen, Julio H. (2004): *The Object of Study in the Humanities*, 1st Edition, Copenhagen: Museum Tusculanums Forlag, ISBN: 9788772898315

Habermas, Jürgen (2015): *The Theory of Communicative Action*, 1st Edition, Cambridge: Polity, ASIN: B016BNHFZW

Habermas, Jürgen (2019a): *Auch eine Geschichte der Philosophie, Band 1: Die okzidentale Konstellation von Glauben und Wissen*, 3rd Edition, Berlin: Suhrkamp Verlag, ISBN: 9783518587348

Habermas, Jürgen (2019b): *Auch eine Geschichte der Philosophie, Band 2: Vernünftige Freiheit. Spuren des Diskurses über Glauben und Wissen*, 3rd Edition, Berlin: Suhrkamp Verlag, ISBN: 9783518587348

Honneth, Axel (1995): Decentered Autonomy: The Subject after the Fall, in: *Fragmented World of the Social: Essays in the Social and Political Philosophy*, 1st Edition, Albany, NY: SUNY Press, ISBN: 079142300X

Horkheimer, Max (2013): *The Eclipse of Reason*, Reprint of 1947 Edition, Eastford, CT: Martino Fine Books, ISBN: 9781614274131

Kaup, Monika (2021): *New Ecological Realism: Post-Apocalyptic Fiction and Contemporary Theory*, 1st Edition, Edinburgh: Edinburgh University Press, ISBN: 9781474483100

Kennedy, Duncan (2014): The Hermeneutic Suspicion in Contemporary American Legal Thought, *Law and Critique*, 25, 91–139 [online], doi: 10.1007/s10978-014-9136-6

Kohn, Margaret (2013): Postcolonialism and Global Justice, *Journal of Global Justice*, 9(3), 187–200 [online], doi: 10.1080/17449626.2013.818459

Korsgaard, Christine (1996): *The Sources of Normativity*, 2nd Edition, Cambridge: Cambridge University Press, ISBN: 9780521559607

Korsgaard, Christine (2008): *The Constitution of Agency: Essays on Practical Reason and Moral Psychology*, 1st Edition, Oxford: Oxford University Press, ISBN: 9780199552740

Korsgaard, Christine (2009): *Self Constitution: Agency, Identity and Integrity*, 1st Edition, New York: Oxford University Press, ISBN: 9780199552801

Kraut, Richard (2018): *The Quality of Life*, 1st Edition, Oxford: Oxford University Press, ISBN: 9780198828846

THE NEW
INSTITUTE

Krull, Wilhelm (Ed.) (2000): *Debates on Issues of Our Common Future*, trans. Helen Schoop, Velbrück Wissenschaft, Weilerswist 2000; German version: *Zukunftsstreit*, ebf. Weilerswist 2000

Krull, Wilhelm (2009): Fostering Competition and Creativity in German and European Higher Education, in: Douglass, John Aubrey; King, C. Judson and Feller, Irwin (2009): *Globalization's Muse: Universities and Higher Education Systems in a Changing World*, Berkeley, CA: Public Policy Press/Center for Studies in Higher Education

Krull, Wilhelm (2011): *Research and Responsibility – Reflections on Our Common Future*, Leipzig: Europäische Verlagsanstalt, ISBN: 978-3-86393-010-3

Krull, Wilhelm (2012): Governance for Integrity and Quality in Universities – Towards a Culture of Creativity and Quality Assurance, *Forschung. Politik – Strategie – Management*, Bielefeld: Universitätsverlag Webler, 3–4, 88–94

Krull, Wilhelm (2014): Auf der Suche nach der integrativen Kraft. Zur Rolle der Geistes- und Sozialwissenschaften in der Universität der Zukunft, lecture at the University of Würzburg, 9 January 2014, published in Theodor-Litt-Jahrbuch 2014/9, 23–41

Krull, Wilhelm (2015): Towards a Culture of Creativity: Reflections on Europe's Striving for Excellence in Research and Innovation, plenary lecture at Congress Center Breslau, 17 September 2013 and *European Review*, 23(1), 12–27

Krull, Wilhelm (2018): Vom Nutzen und Nachteil der Geisteswissenschaften für das Leben in einer technisch geprägten Welt, lecture at Leibniz University Hannover on the occasion of the 'Tag der Philosophischen Fakultät' on 24 November 2016, Logbuch der Philosophischen Fakultät PHILOSOVIEL, 2018, 22–31

Latour, Bruno (2009): *Das Parlament der Dinge – Für eine politische Ökologie*, 5th Edition, Berlin: Suhrkamp, ISBN 978-3-518-29554-0

Leiter, Brian (2010): Foundations of Religious Liberty: Toleration or Respect?, *San Diego Law Review*, 47(4), 935, https://digital.sandiego.edu/sdlr/vol47/iss4/5

Leiter, Brian (2013): *Why Tolerate Religion?*, 4th Edition, Princeton, NJ: Princeton University Press, ISBN: 9780691153612

Lévi-Strauss, Claude (2004): *Anthropologie structurale Deux*, Paris: Pocket, ISBN: 9782266140034

TOWARDS A NEW ENLIGHTENMENT ■ MARKUS GABRIEL, CHRISTOPH HORN, ANNA KATSMAN, WILHELM KRULL, ANNA LUISA LIPPOLD, CORINE PELLUCHON, INGO VENZKE

71

Lima de Miranda, Katharina and Snower, Dennis J. (2020): Recoupling Economic and Social Prosperity, in: *CESifo Working Papers*, 8133, 1–46 [online], doi: https://doi.org/10.2139/ssrn.3548365

Litt, Theodor (1926): *Individuum und Gemeinschaft: Grundlegung der Kulturphilosophie*, 1st Edition, Leipzig: Teubner, ASIN: B002EIIHE2

Luhrmann, Tanya, M. (2020): *How God Becomes Real: Kindling the Presence of Invisible Others*, 1st Edition, Princeton, NJ: Princeton University Press, ISBN: 9780691164465

Lyotard, Jean-Francois (1984): *The Postmodern Condition: A Report on Knowledge*, 1st Edition, Manchester: Manchester University Press, ISBN: 9780719014505

Madsbjerg, Christian (2017): *Sensemaking: The Power of Humanities in the Age of the Algorithm*, 1st Edition, London: Hachette Books, ISBN: 978140870836.1

Merleau-Ponty, Maurice (1960): *De Mauss à Levi-Strauss, Gallimard*, Paris: Signes, ISBN: 2-07-024427

Merleau-Ponty, Maurice (1983): *Structure of Behavior*, Pittsburgh, PA: Duquesne University Press, ISBN: 9780820701639

Mulgan, Geoff (2021): *The Case for Exploratory Social Sciences*, Hamburg: THE NEW INSTITUTE [online], https://thenew.institute/en/media/the-case-for-exploratory-social-sciences

Mulgan, Geoff (2022): *Another World Is Possible: How to Reignite Social and Political Imagination*, 1st Edition, London: C. Hurst & Co. Publishers Ltd, ISBN: 9781787386914

Nagel, Thomas (1989): *The View from Nowhere*, 1st Edition, Oxford: Oxford University Press, ISBN: 9780195056440

Nakajima, Takahiro (2021): *Capitalism and Human Co-Becoming*, 1st Edition, Tokyo: University of Tokyo Press, ISBN: 9784130130981

Nathan, Otto and Horden, Heinz (1960): *Einstein on Peace*, 1st Edition, New York: Simon & Schuster

Nussbaum, Martha C. (2016): *Not for Profit: Why Democracy Needs the Humanities*, Revised Edition, Princeton, NJ: Princeton University Press, ISBN: 9780691173320

Ober, Josiah (2010): *Democracy and Knowledge: Innovation and Learning in Classical Athens*, New Edition, Princeton, NJ: Princeton University Press, ISBN: 9780691146249

Ophir, Adi (2005): *The Order of Evils: Toward an Ontology of Morals*, 1st English Edition, Princeton, NJ: Princeton University Press, ISBN: 9781890951511

Parfit, Derek (2011): *On What Matters*, 1st Edition, Oxford: Oxford University Press, ISBN: 978-0199681044

Pelluchon, Corine (2019): *Nourishment: A Philosophy of the Political Body*, trans. J. E. Smith, London: Bloomsbury, ISBN: 978-2070170944

Pelluchon, Corine (2020): *Réparons le monde: Humains, animaux, nature*, 1st Edition, Paris: RIVAGES, ISBN: 9782743649982

Pelluchon, Corine (2021a): *Les Lumières à l'âge du vivant*, 1st Edition, Paris: Seuil, ISBN: 978-2021425017

Pelluchon, Corine (2021b): Ecology as a New Enlightenment, *Global Solutions Journal, The World Policy Forum*, 7, 218–223 [online], hal-03240808

Pelluchon, Corine (2022, forthcoming): *Ricœur, Philosophe de la reconstruction: Soin, attestation, justice*, Paris: PUF, ISBN 978-2130827207

Putnam, Hilary (1981): *Reason, Truth and History*, 1st Edition, Cambridge: Cambridge University Press, ISBN: 9780511625398

Putnam, Hilary (2004): *The Collapse of the Fact/Value Dichotomy and Other Essays*, 3rd Edition, Cambridge, MA: Harvard University Press, ISBN: 9780674013803

Railton, Peter (2003): *Facts, Values and Norms: Essays Towards a Morality of Consequence*, 1st Edition, Cambridge: Cambridge University Press, ISBN: 9780511613982

Ricœur, Paul (1992): *Oneself as Another*, 1st Edition, Chicago, IL: University of Chicago Press, ISBN: 9780226713298

Ricœur, Paul (2008): *Freud and Philosophy: An Essay on Interpretation*, 1st Edition, Delhi: Motilal Banarsidass Publishers, ISBN: 9788120833050

Riskin, Jessica (2016): *The Restless Clock: A History of the Centuries-Long Argument over What Makes Living Things Tick*, 1st Edition, Chicago, IL: University of Chicago Press, ISBN: 9780226528267

Rosa, Hartmut (2021): Best Account: Skizze einer systematischen Theorie der modernen Gesellschaft, in: Reckwitz, Andreas and Rosa, Hartmut (2021): *Spätmoderne in der Krise: Was leistet die Gesellschaftstheorie*, 2nd Edition, Berlin: Suhrkamp Verlag, ISBN: 9783518587751

Russell, Stuart J. (2019): *Human Compatible: Artificial Intelligence and the Problem of Control*, 1st Edition, London: Allen Lane. ISBN: 9780525558613

Sartre, Jean-Paul (2007): *Existentialism Is a Humanism*, Annotated Edition, New Haven, CT: Yale University Press, ISBN: 9780300115468

TOWARDS A NEW ENLIGHTENMENT ■ MARKUS GABRIEL,
CHRISTOPH HORN, ANNA KATSMAN, WILHELM KRULL,
ANNA LUISA LIPPOLD, CORINE PELLUCHON, INGO VENZKE

73

Scanlon, Thomas, M. (2000): *What We Owe to Each Other*, 1st Edition, Cambridge, MA: Harvard University Press, ISBN: 9780674004238

Scanlon, Thomas M. (2014): *Being Realistic about Reason*, 1st Edition, Oxford: Oxford University Press, ISBN: 9780199678488

Sen, Amartya K. (1977): Rational Fools: A Critique of the Behavioral Foundations of Economic Theory, *Philosophy & Public Affairs*, 6(4), 317–344 [online], http://www.jstor.org/stable/2264946

Shafer-Landau, Russ (2003): *Moral Realism: A Defence*, 1st Edition, Oxford: Oxford University Press, ISBN: 9780199259755

Spivak, Gayatri, C. (1999): *A Critique of Postcolonial Thought: Toward a History of Vanishing Past*, 1st Edition, Cambridge, MA: Harvard University Press, ISBN: 9780674177642

Spivak, Gayatri, C. (2007): *Can the Subaltern Speak?*, 1st Edition, Vienna: Turia and Kant, ISBN: 9783851325065

Sternhell, Zeev (2009): *The Anti-Enlightenment Tradition*, trans. D. Maisel, New Haven, CT: Yale University Press, ISBN: 978-0300135541

Srinivasan, Amia (2019): Genealogy, Epistemology and Worldmaking, *Proceedings of the Aristotelian Society*, 119(2), 127–156, [online] doi: 10.1093/arisoc/aoz009

Stanley, Jason (2016): *How Propaganda Works*, Reprint Edition, Princeton, NJ: Princeton University Press, ISBN: 9780691173429

Taylor, Charles (1985): *Human Agency and Language: Philosophical Papers Volume 1*, 1st Edition, Cambridge: Cambridge University Press. ISBN: 9780521267526

Venzke, Ingo (2016): Crackling the Frame? On the Prospects of Change in a World of Struggle, *European Journal of International Law*, 27(3), 831–851 [online], doi: 10.1093/ejil/chw036

Venzke, Ingo (2022): The Practice of Interpretation in International Law: Strategies of Critique, in: Dunoff, Jeffrey L. and Pollack, Mark A. (2022): *International Legal Theory: Foundations and Frontiers*, Cambridge: Cambridge University Press, ISBN: 9781108427715

Weber, Max (1904): Objektivität sozialwissenschaftlicher und sozialpolitischer Erkenntnis: in: Weber, Max (1988): *Gesammelte Aufsätze zur Wissenschaftslehre*, 1st Edition. Tübingen: J.C.B. Mohr, ISBN: 9783825214920

Weber, Max (1918): Wissenschaft als Beruf, in: Weber, Max (1988): *Gesammelte Aufsätze zur Wissenschaftslehre*, 1st Edition. Tübingen: J.C.B. Mohr, ISBN: 9783825214920

Weber, Max (1988): *Gesammelte Aufsätze zur Wissenschaftslehre*, 1st Edition. Tübingen: J. C. B. Mohr, ISBN: 9783825214920

White, Lynn (1976): The Historical Roots of Our Ecological Crisis, *Science*, 155, 1203–1207, doi: 10.1126/science.155.3767.1203

Zeuske, Michael (2018): *Sklaverei: Eine Menschheitsgeschichte von der Steinzeit bis heute*, 2nd Edition, Stuttgart: Reclam. ISBN: 9783150111550

Zhao, Tingyang (2021): *All under Heaven: The Tianxia System for a Possible World Order*, Oakland, CA: University of California Press, ISBN: 9780520325029; first published in a Chinese version: 天下的当代性: 世界秩序的实践与想象, China CITIC Press (2016), ISBN: 9787508656717

TOWARDS A NEW ENLIGHTENMENT ■ MARKUS GABRIEL,
CHRISTOPH HORN, ANNA KATSMAN, WILHELM KRULL,
ANNA LUISA LIPPOLD, CORINE PELLUCHON, INGO VENZKE

75

About the authors

Markus Gabriel is academic director at THE NEW INSTITUTE and interim chair of its programme "The Foundations of Value and Values". He holds the chair for epistemology, modern and contemporary philosophy at Rheinische Friedrich-Wilhelms-Universität Bonn.

Christoph Horn is a professor at Rheinische Friedrich-Wilhelms-Universität Bonn and holds the chair for practical philosophy and ancient philosophy. He was a fellow at THE NEW INSTITUTE in 2021/22.

Anna Katsman is academic director at THE NEW INSTITUTE and was a fellow in 2021/22. She holds a PhD in philosophy from the New School for Social Research in New York.

Wilhelm Krull is the founding director at THE NEW INSTITUTE and was general secretary of the Volkswagen Foundation for more than 20 years. He holds numerous leading positions in national and international supervisory and advisory bodies.

Anna Luisa Lippold is the manager of the programme "The Foundations of Value and Values" at THE NEW INSTITUTE. She holds a PhD in applied ethics from the Ruhr-Universität Bochum.

Corine Pelluchon is a professor of philosophy at the Université Gustave Eiffel, a statutory member of the Hannah Arendt Interdisciplinary Laboratory for Political Studies, and a fellow at THE NEW INSTITUTE in 2021/22 and 2022/23.

Ingo Venzke is a professor of international law and social justice at Universiteit van Amsterdam and Director of the Amsterdam Center for International Law (ACIL). He is a fellow at THE NEW INSTITUTE in 2021/22 and 2022/23.

THE NEW
INSTITUTE

THE NEW
INSTITUTE

www.thenew.institute